SURVIVORS and *Thrivers*

Male homosexual lives in postwar Australia

DAVID GOULD

Queer oz Folk is produced on the land of
the Wurundjeri people of the Kulin Nation.
We acknowledge the Traditional Owners of country
throughout Australia and recognise their
continuing connection to land, waters and culture.
We pay our respects to their Elders past, present and emerging.
Their land was stolen, never ceded.
It always was and always will be Aboriginal land.

To be a homosexual is to wear a mask all the time
– Peter Wildeblood, giving evidence to the Departmental Committee on Homosexual Offences and Prostitution (Wolfenden Committee), UK, 1954

For the men who survived – and for those who did not.

In memory of my parents, Rita and Keith Gould and of Alan

First published 2023 by Interventions Inc
PO Box 963 Coffs Harbour
NSW, Australia 2450

Interventions is a not-for-profit, independent, radical book publisher.
 For further information:
   www.interventions.org.au
   info@interventions.org.au

Queer Oz Folk Series Vol 4
Series editor: Graham Willett
Queer Oz Folk publishes Australian queer history in good quality, affordable editions with an eye to the widest possible audiences.

Cover and text design: Cathy Larsen, www.cathylarsendesign.com
Front cover photo: Dennis Myall and friends, Courtesy Dennis Mayall

Author: David Gould

Title: Survivors and thrivers: Male homosexual lives in postwar Australia
ISBN: 978-0-6452535-2-8 Paperback
ISBN: 978-0-6452535-3-5 ebook

© David Gould 2023

The moral rights of the author have been asserted.
All rights reserved. Except as permitted under the Australian Copyright Act 1968 (for example, a fair dealing for the purposes of study, research, criticism or review), no part of this book may be reproduced, stored in a retrieval system, communicated or transmitted in any form or by any means without prior written permission.

All inquiries should be made to the author.

 A catalogue record for this book is available from the National Library of Australia

Contents

1. What have we overlooked? — 1
2. Defining 'homosexual': Legal, medical, and psychiatric interventions — 9
3. Constructing 'homosexual': Integration of self — 45
4. Navigating 'homosexual': Family and Marriage — 81
5. Embracing 'homosexual': Finding the men — 118
6. So now we know — 179
   Endnotes — 189
   Interviewees — 197
   Picture credits — 203
   Index — 204

1

What have we overlooked?

Silences of the past

'It will never be fully accepted'. Scott, the man who inspired this book, spoke those words some time ago, aged 87. He passed away in February 2019, but his words and his history remain here. His declaration seemed to me to include an intangible complexity, deeply felt emotion, sadness, inevitability but also defiance that, together, summarised a life of learning. 'It' of course, referred to homosexuality. Yet, contrary to the suggestion of rejection and struggle in the above words, Scott always entertained me with his subversive and surprisingly upbeat stories of the postwar years as a homosexual living in Melbourne. There had to be more to this history! The interest, the shock, the laughter, the pain and the joy within Scott's narratives told me that his history – our homosexual history, and therefore Australian history of the era – was holding back its secrets. The complexities of homosexual lives in the 1940s and 1950s somehow had not seemed important enough for thorough research and recognition. Homosexual men (and women) were approaching the end of their lives without our ever having acknowledged or celebrated their survival. Silently, they had gifted to all of us their experience, resilience and compassion. In generations past, they had opened a pathway towards gay liberation decades later; yet, few of us really comprehended the enormity of their offering or took a moment to listen. It is time to bridge this gap in history.

How extraordinary it must seem to homosexuals who were young adults in the 1940s and 1950s that, in 2018, I was able to marry my partner of 25 years. In my speech on the day, I listed the terms that interviewees for this book recalled as designating a 'homosexual', including: 'that dreaded word poofter'; 'mortal sin'; 'a police matter'; 'queen'; 'effeminate'; 'undesirable'; 'deplorable'; 'almost the street walker'; 'not being a proper man'; 'pansy'; and 'took the wrong turning'. They were also called 'not worth very much'; 'not very intelligent'; and 'the lowest of the low'. One interviewee, describing what it was like to be a homosexual in the era, recalled:

> you certainly couldn't tell your parents, because you can't tell your parents you're a terrible criminal who is liable to go to jail.
> I knew I was going to be on my own.

What was this history? Why hadn't it been told? What were its complexities? What were its joys? What impact did institutions such as the family, marriage, religion, the law, medicine and society have on them? In short, how had men survived? And what could this history tell us about ourselves, our society and our country? Even today, homosexual history is concerned with filling gaps. Whereas 1970s gay and lesbian theory concentrated on 'the historical emergence or invention of the homosexual', queer theory in the 1990s was more concerned with institutional constraints on homosexual behaviour. But gay historian Jeffrey Weeks warns that history can fall into the trap of only considering the structures or forces that determine how something is defined, rather than examining agency within lived experience.[1] We need to question and explain diversity of sexual experience; origins and practice of power; and the multiplicity of different social worlds.

This book aims to address structure, agency *and* lived realities. It exposes the practice of structured power by examining its presentation and impact on homosexual lives. It also reveals how homosexual men succumbed to, accommodated or resisted that power, exploring the psychological mindset that prevented or permitted those reactions. Lastly, it documents and offers explanations of their lived experience at a micro level, because that is where the impacts of structure and agency played out. In doing so, it uncovers history that has not had a voice.

Old and new voices

The stories and the new history contained in this book came directly from one-on-one interviews with 27 men who responded to my public request for volunteers. The youngest was 74 and the oldest 95. All were aged at least 16 in the year following the end of the war. All were white males, selected on the basis that they identified as homosexual and that they had lived in Australia for most or all of the postwar era. I use the term 'gay' in reference to contemporary times, but 'homosexual' otherwise, because 'gay' postdates the history covered within this book. Interviewees also used 'camp' once or twice, but most notable was the absence of any affirming language that described homosexuality at the time. In fact, the men often confirmed that the term 'homosexual' was not used among homosexuals. They were more likely to identify another homosexual by a nod of the head – in itself a form of silencing of homosexual existence.

Their stories acknowledge and clarify further the dark recesses of our homosexual past; but they also boldly celebrate lives that were neither completely repressed nor totally invisible. At a time when homosexuals were viewed as mentally deficient, morally repugnant and a threat to national security and nation building, homosexual men still found ways to endure by living 'under the radar' of the general population's scrutiny. These men were 'survivors' because they managed to exist within a rigidly heteronormative society while still finding ways to nurture contact with other homosexual men – with varying degrees of success. The struggle to understand what it meant to be homosexual involved adept management of information about themselves in order to avoid questions from school mates, family members, work colleagues, police, doctors, psychologists and ministers of religion. Fear, shame and confusion about sexual desire added to the complexity of 'passing' as heterosexual in society while guarding a potentially destructive secret. One man described the fear: 'you were now terribly aware. Is there a policeman on our radar?... it was total control and awareness... and putting panic into you'.

The stories in this book shift beyond the struggle and the anonymity that many homosexual men lived with because almost one-third belonged to a second grouping – the 'thrivers'. These men embraced their homosexual identity and 'passed' in society by being informed and agile in their responses to heterosexual expectations. In place of shame and fear, they harnessed their own self-belief and accepted their homosexuality in a pragmatic, enthusiastic manner – still within the confines of heterosexual society. They did more than simply exist 'under the radar': they connected with homosexual 'communities'; they created extensive homosexual friendship networks; they enjoyed homosexual gatherings at pubs and in private parties; and they had lots of sex!

At the heart of this book is the question of how these men lived 'under the radar' and what the implications of that were for their wellbeing and the conduct of their everyday lives. Their stories unpeel the complex layers that overlaid their lives, enabling us to better understand their experience and what that says about our collective

The two faces of Robert Albert Lott/Lottie

history. With them, we examine the process of realisation of homosexuality and its impacts on the individual's life – including the confusion of trying either to incorporate or to *appear* to incorporate the self into a foreign (heterosexual) identity, while at the same time grappling with a reassessment and readjustment of the (homosexual) self.

In the postwar period, two institutions central to this tension were the family and marriage. This book examines the responses to difference of the people involved, their influence on the men's struggle and the ways in which homosexual men managed heteronormative cultural inheritance. It then shifts to the question of desire. How did these men accommodate their need for physical and emotional contact with other men within a system that proscribed such eroticism? Progressively and surreptitiously, homosexual men accumulated knowledge about themselves and about their communities. They passed on this knowledge to other homosexuals, so that they too could survive. Significantly, it was the degree of a man's homosexual cultural knowledge that most often determined whether he became a 'survivor' or a 'thriver'.

Those who could add to our knowledge of our postwar past were of advanced age, creating a sense of urgency about recording this history before it was lost forever. Over 40 years ago, Katz argued that 'modern' homosexual identity had moved from a 'personal and devastating fate, a private, secret shame' to a 'consciousness of ourselves as members of an oppressed social group'.[2] This book examines how men in the 1940s and 1950s began and developed this process of self re-education, how they reimagined 'truth' and what it meant to be homosexual. The men's collective history charts complex incremental shifts in Australian attitudes about exclusion and inclusion; acceptance of difference and rejection of otherness; individual identity and national character; familial connectivity and the straining of blood bonds; shame and oppression; and the place of sexuality (especially alternative sexualities) in the national psyche. Their narratives attest to a diversity of experience that disrupts any single, uniform account of how lives were lived. Instead, it commands attention to the details of their lives and the way in which they, individually and collectively, accommodated, challenged or succumbed to contemporary belief systems and structures. The experiences of these men provide an immediate, intimate and human bridging of history that deepens our sense of how we have moved from 1940s and 1950s homosexual censure and criminality, through the sexual awakening, struggle and liberation of the 1960s, 1970s and 1980s, and on to contemporary times, with gay marriage, adoption rights, and days such as IDAHOBIT (International Day Against Homophobia, Biphobia and Transphobia). This book, therefore, helps to connect the work of Wayne Murdoch's recent *Kamp Melbourne in the 1920s and '30s: Trade, queans and inverts*, and Graham Willett's more recent and celebratory *Living out loud*.

Postwar Australian society and homosexuality

The reader should examine these stories with postwar belief systems about homosexuality front of mind. In 1940s and 1950s Australia, homosexual men had to conceal their true selves to survive, to avoid shame, to retain employment, to avoid imprisonment and to maintain respect. This suppression of a fundamental part of one's personality had profound impacts on individuals and on homosexuals as a group. Commonly, it curtailed opportunities for men to reach their full personal potential and to live openly and joyfully. At its most powerful, it ruined lives; in some cases, it ended them.

Homosexual men knew that they were outsiders, often before they even acknowledged their same-sex attraction.[3] Describing the development of their own sexual knowledge, almost every interviewee uttered the same words: 'I knew I was different'. Often, this understanding occurred around the age of six (incidentally, the age of beginning school). By the time they were teenagers, they were aware of the stigma attached to homosexuality, even if its meanings eluded them.

Such messages were conveyed through language that characterised homosexuals as effeminate – 'queens', 'sissies', or 'pansies' – or as sub-normal outsiders – 'poofters' or 'queers'. Often, close family members or friends communicated these attitudes. Many homosexuals felt fear and shame because they were not what their families expected them to be. Further, their 'failings' as males meant that their families would also feel shame and could not be proud of their sons.

Figuratively and literally, homosexuals had no 'place' within society. Despite the negative connotations attached to it, there is little evidence that homosexuality was discussed in 1940s and 1950s Australia– publicly or privately. The men in this book reported never hearing the subject or the word mentioned. Even within homosexual friendship groups, the word 'homosexual' was not used. Instead, homosexuals became adept at reading body language.

Homosexual men as a group were, therefore, fragmented. There were those with some knowledge of homosexuality and those with barely any. This meant that relatively small numbers of homosexual men were ever together at one time. They could not talk with each other about their experience of being homosexual. Most were too caught up with surviving and avoiding exposure to be building a homosexual community. So, the question remains: where were the other homosexual survivors? The answer is that they remained silently ensconced in the heterosexual world that despised them. For most, although not all, this had a significant impact on their emotional wellbeing; their enjoyment of life; their sense of self; their relationships with friends and family; their choice of work and the behaviours they displayed at work; their public persona versus their private, inner life; their social life; their choices about major life decisions (such as marriage); and, ultimately, their mental and physical health. Anecdotally, there were also other homosexual men who succumbed to more destructive responses to their homosexuality – such as alcoholism and suicide.

This book draws on the concept of 'struggle' as being central to what homosexual men were doing in the 1940s and 1950s. Homosexuals wrestled with regulation, prejudice and punishment. They searched for a safe and affirming place in society. And they longed for the support of others like them. Homosexual gatherings occurred in a few hotels and at private parties among the more confident and informed; but, even for these men, experiencing this sense of solidarity and community could only be possible at certain times and places. This alternative 'identity' was often not publicly or privately acknowledged as a sexual identity. Once they returned home to parents and family, workplaces or public lives, their homosexual selves were again silenced. Even so, this homosexual history is more complex than a study of repudiation. Men did find ways to survive, while a much smaller number thrived. Through their stories, we can unpeel the layers that explain exactly how they did so.

A final note on terminology. The term 'homosexual' was first used in 1869. Prior to that, descriptors of male homosexuals included 'sodomite', 'nancy', 'molly', 'queen', 'poofter' and 'invert'.[4] By the early 20th century, 'camp' or 'kamp' was also used, until 'gay' became the preferred term from the early 1970s. Earlier lexicon emphasised the supposedly effeminate and unnatural sex acts of homosexuals and highlighted a sense of missing masculinity. In contrast, in Australia in the 1950s, 'camp' was simply a term used by homosexual men to describe themselves. By the time 'gay' was in common usage from the 1970s, the meaning of homosexuality had shifted from a description of characteristics or sexual acts to an overt cultural construct that began to celebrate its otherness.[5] It is this cultural dimension to the word 'gay' that prompts contemporary homosexuals to prefer the term to the more medicalised sense of 'homosexual'. Given the postwar positioning of the history in this book, however, 'homosexual' is used throughout (unless in a direct quote). From the date of their foundation, the late 19th century Australian colonies (and later states) had incorporated British laws into their own legal frameworks and declared male homosexual sex illegal.[6] It took almost another 100 years before Tasmania became the last Australian state to decriminalise homosexual acts between consenting adults, in 1997.[7]

2

Defining 'homosexual': Legal, medical, and psychiatric interventions

The Law

Rodney Croome has argued that anti-homosexual sentiment began in Australia during its convict era. Authorities not only found sexual relations between men morally repugnant; they also viewed close emotional bonds between convicts as a threat to their authority. It was harder to maintain discipline if men were prepared to protect lovers, no matter the cost.[1] A century and a half later in 1940s and 1950s Australia, attitudes and laws about sex had changed little. Based on Christian beliefs, sexuality and sexual expression were viewed as heterosexual – and morally acceptable only if practised within marriage and for the purpose of creating new life. Laws that outlawed homosexual sex criminalised its practice but also fomented prejudice that allowed police and others to freely intimidate, blackmail, entrap and abuse suspected homosexuals.[2] The impact thus created both a private and public existential threat for homosexuals.

The belief systems that shaped laws on homosexual sex inform how and why they existed. By criminalising sexual relations between men, the laws reinforced the 'role of family, marriage, children, childhood, and parental authority'.[3] They also helped to define gender expectations and sexual identity. Homosexuals posed a risk to the social order and undermined the country's desire to rebuild after World War II. With the law on their side, and encouraged by state sanctioned bigotry, police in the 1950s (particularly in New South Wales) mounted sustained campaigns to rid society of the 'homosexual menace'. An unexpected outcome of this intimidation was that the public became more aware of the questionable techniques used by police to arrest homosexuals.[4] But, although homosexuals could theoretically challenge these approaches in court, doing so risked public exposure and, if found guilty, imprisonment.

Such history provides context as to why it took almost another half century before all Australian states had finally decriminalised homosexual sex. Further, it highlights the historic significance of the 24 May 2016 Victorian Government apology to homosexual men who had been convicted under anti-homosexual laws.[5] This was the first such apology in any jurisdiction in the world. It recognised that, in order to understand discrimination against minority groups, we need to look further than difference in treatment. At the core of prejudicial practice are laws and the people who impose them to reproduce and strengthen the status quo.[6] All the men in this book who had encounters with the law, the courts or the police because of their homosexuality during the postwar era reported negative experiences that manifested from adverse responses to their sexuality. The impacts of those experiences were uniformly damaging and often life changing.

Policing deplorables

Entrapment, raids and consequences: Francis' story

Francis, 80, provided a singular perspective of the policing of homosexuals in postwar Australia, because he himself was a policeman in Queensland at the time. He recounted one story that illustrated the pervasive danger homosexuals faced and the possibility of arrest or blackmail:

> When I was a very young copper, about 19, I was sent to work at the watch-house, which was so tough and so rough, and there was an extremely good-looking young copper there, who was very nice to me and helpful to me. A few days later he was arrested because what he was doing, there was another famous pickup joint, North Key. He [the good-looking young copper] was a married man. He went over to North Key, propositioned

this guy, and when the guy grabbed his dick, told him it was going to cost him £50. And the guy went to the police, and the policeman's defence was 'Well, everybody's doing it'.

What is especially noteworthy in Francis' story is that the victim actually reported the incident to the police, probably in 1956, so it is possible that he had taken confidence from the 1953 court appeals brought by men who had been charged with soliciting. The judge in one of those appeals had ruled that police had fabricated evidence against homosexual men, noting that there was no evidence to prove guilt and thereby establishing doubts about police methods in entrapping homosexuals. In the second case, a judge ruled that soliciting laws used against homosexuals only applied if one male invited another to have sex with a female prostitute.[7] The second revealing detail in Francis' story is important because the 'young copper' acknowledges that such entrapment and blackmail is common among the police at the time. A third observation is that he apparently believes that his attempt at blackmail should be excused because other police were illegally threatening homosexuals with arrest if they did not hand over money. The victim who reported him displayed courage and probably clearly understood interpretations of law. It is also likely that there were many, many other homosexuals who had no such agency; for them, the only option was to pay up.

Francis also described a police raid on homosexuals. He considers himself 'very, very fortunate' to be the person who 'told the story', rather than a protagonist in it:

> Surfers Paradise at that time had a lot of old homes in it – it was before all the, all the high-rises, and there was a group of about 10 people, mostly professionals, having a little party and at the time I was going out with a champion lifesaver in Queensland who drove a big Jaguar sports car, and I was sitting on the stair waiting for him to come and I saw a police car pull up and all these detectives spill out, so I ran through the house yelling out 'The police are here!' and I ran, got away, and it was written up in

> Brisbane *Telegraph* [newspaper]: 'A Nest of Perverts Discovered'.[8]
> Two of them were very good doctors, a couple were barristers I think – all they were doing was having a drink!

The consequences of being caught could range from having your name recorded, as a homosexual person of interest, to arrest, depending on the decisions of the arresting police. Francis had his own theories about the motivations of police at the time:

> D: And were they arrested?
>
> F: Well, their names were taken and then of course, if they ever, if they were ever questioned again you were gone.
>
> D: And can you, can you pinpoint, what was it that, why were the police so interested in homosexuals?
>
> F: Well, you get all various types of police. First of all, you get the man that joins the police to help the world, the ones you see on television.
>
> Then you get the people that are slightly misfits, and they join the police to have the power. Then you have the police who are very, very keen for a promotion, so, he is the detective in charge, it would be Surfers Paradise and quite a bit of other territory in those days, and if he can discover this nest of perverts and save the world, all the better. And when it got in *The Truth* – all the better!
>
> It would go on his record, so when the Promotions' Board met, they would see it, and think 'Well, this man's got a bit of gumption'.
>
> D: What happened to the men whose names were written up in *Truth?*
>
> F: Well, I can't remember. They put their names – they put that they were a nest of perverts. Well, they just got on with

Defining 'homosexual': Legal, medical, and psychiatric interventions

doctoring, or hairdressing or whatever they were doing. What were they going to do? But they would have had to have been 100% more careful.

Perhaps this particular group of men was fortunate in presenting as the professional men they were; but their close escape from arrest would have been not only frightening, but also an ongoing threat to their professional careers. It is not hard to imagine that many such men would have become very aware of such police raids and, therefore, would be careful to plan only private homosexual social gatherings and to be meticulous in their choice of guests, the time and place they were held, how access was granted and what they would do if police turned up. In contemporary times, it is extraordinary to think that homosexual men were forced to take such precautions to have a private dinner party together.

For homosexuals who were unfortunate enough to be charged, the law could be brutal. Francis recalled friends whose stories illustrated just how damaging it was to their lives:

D: Did you know anyone who went to court? Had to go to court? Charged?

F: Oh, yes! I was sitting in the Supreme Court and saw a dear friend of mine who was sitting near, and he was locked up I think for 7 years.

D: 7 years?! For what?

F: Oh, buggery or something. And in those days, there was no District Court in Brisbane. You either have Petty Sessions or the Supreme Court, so it was in this huge, magnificent courtroom with the judge sitting up on the podium in scarlet. There was no black cap because there was no death [penalty], but he was carted away, and of course he would have been, once he settled down in jail he would have been alright though.

Those who escaped conviction still had to face the shame of being charged and making a court appearance. Often, the impact was almost as devastating as jail:

> D: And do you know any men who were charged and but, perhaps went to jail, but at least charged – the impact that it had on their lives?
>
> F: Well, it's horrific. I had a great friend, and he was arrested in King George Square, and he was a lovely man. He had some big job, might have been a teacher or something, but he lost his job. You'd lose your job automatically... and of course, if they had caught me, well, I would have lost my job too.
>
> D: And the men who lost their jobs, what did they do afterwards? How did they live?
>
> F: Well, they sort of disappeared. Generally, they went to Sydney.
>
> D: Right, right. So, they would have to leave their state and start a new life?
>
> F: They had to relocate because, it's a bit like now, like if you see, when you watch these shows on television about customs, if you're questioned once, every time you come through customs after that they will pull you up.
>
> D: Right.
>
> F: So, the same thing applies – if you were arrested once, the next time there would be no leeway. They would grab you every time because they'd put you up in front of a magistrate, he'd convict you because you already had form.
>
> D: Yes. And what about the families of those men, what was the response?
>
> F: Well, what could they say? They were in shock.

Surprisingly, Francis recalled that 'generally', families did not reject their sons afterwards but remained supportive of them, thus sharing in the shame and damage to reputations.

From burglary to buggery: Stephen's story

Stephen, 79, offered a unique insight into the policing of homosexuals and their treatment in court, because he was a journalist on a newspaper in Warrnambool, a large Victorian town, during the postwar period. He 'used to have to go and report the [Magistrate's] courts, just every Tuesday usually'. He particularly recalled the case of one man because of the way police took advantage of the man's naïveté to obtain information about him that led to his immediate arrest, despite his initial interview being totally unrelated to homosexual acts. Even more shocking was the extraordinary intimacy of the questioning he endured during his court appearance. Stephen described:

> a young man, he worked for the shoe shop, he was a shoe-shop assistant, I think. He was in Warrnambool, yeah, he was charged, charged that between such and such a date, and such and such a date 'You did commit the abominable crime of buggery', which as you may know that was the case. And, and then they had to, and I'm sitting there and I'm learning, learning about what a case like this involved because I remember his pyjamas and his friend got him to take the pyjama trousers off or something. But anyway, the cross-examination had to go very particular – now 'Was he?', 'Was it hard?', 'How hard was it?', you know, and all that detail – the state of his penis and so on, and whether he liked it or not. Or you know, 'How did it go in?', 'How far did it go in?' Oh, yeah, all that detail had to be in the court and you know, people writing down and ... well, that was a bit of a, that was the first one I'd come across of one of those, ah, details, and even, and the detectives had originally talked to this young guy over a burglary or something like that, you see and so, they covered that, and then they said, 'Now is there anything else you'd like

to chat, get off your chest and talk to us about?', you know and
they were using, they're very good at all that stuff [interrogating].
So that's how that [was] revealed. Well after that we went out [of
the court] and he [editor] said 'We won't use that story'.

Stephen could not recall what sentence was passed but he did 'remember being a bit aghast at the detail'. It is a revealing story that tells us much about the interpretation and practice of law during the era and the degree to which due legal process, as we now understand it, was absent. Unsurprisingly, the experience left Stephen conscious that the case:

reveal[ed] the sort of attitude to things because... it was all highly
illegal so therefore my attitude during this period, all that time,
I was very conscious of the fact, you know, not breaking the law.

Arrest and confession: Herbert's story

Herbert, 87, lives with his long-term partner in suburban Melbourne. After leaving school at the age of 16, he initially worked in a confectionary warehouse as a storeman but 'realised I wasn't too good at it', so management asked him to go into sales. This didn't change much, however, because all he 'ended up doing was lumping stuff away into their vans and their trucks'. Fortunately, a client of his father's suggested that Herbert should apply for a job with the Education Department in the Visual Education unit at 'Melbourne Tech' (later RMIT). At 17, he began as a 'rewind boy', rewinding film. Over the next six years, he: 'learned everything to do with visual aids', including 'projectors and projection, [about] being a librarian, how to file, cut and edit film'. During this time, Herbert 'realised how much I loved screening films'. He became a projectionist and later 'taught motion picture projection'.

At 18, Herbert was conscripted into the 'first national army service' – 'an enormous shock to the system as a fellow who had never been away from home'. He recalled:

the only thing that got me through that was, interestingly

enough, at night, I realised that I was very different to the guys I was with. They were far more interested in sport, horse-racing, what women they could get out with and all the rest of it, and the sex that went along in their minds and vocally. And then they were not interested in any subjects at all!

When he left the army at around 20, he felt 'a great relief, yet strangely enough found that I was very lonely'. He decided that, because 'I was always interested in dancing' and had 'already done a bit of classical ballet', he would take on teaching dance at 'Arthur Murray's ballroom dancing'. He coupled this with his 'love of playing the ukulele, song and dance'. Eventually, he 'couldn't see myself ever earning money being a song and dance man' and knew he needed 'something more substantial', so he 'contacted [his] friend who was with the ABC, now in its second year of television, just after the Olympics'. That contact asked Herbert whether he 'would like to join him at the ABC and I said, "Would I!" So, I started my life in television!'

It was a happy period of Herbert's life. He was:

> with a whole crowd of people whom I enjoyed being with very much because we were the pioneers of television. It was the old black and white television and I was there for about three years.

Herbert aspired to be 'a writer and producer of film'. In his role as film librarian, he met 'a fellow from the Shell Oil Company' and was invited to go for an interview at the Shell film unit. He soon learned that the unit was to be disbanded, so he was counselled to consider television commercials production. Shell had a 'very big advertising agency'. Consequently, in his early 20s, Herbert found himself 'learning from the people [he] was working with all about commercials and writing commercials and also jingles'. He 'was very grateful for those years because it made me realise how I could work my creative sense'. Then 'halfway through working for that agency there came an opportunity to do live television at GTV9, Channel 7 and all the commercial stations', and Herbert became a 'junior producer for live television'.

Work at GTV9 was a pivotal time for Herbert for other reasons. He recalled that:

> One of the copywriters I realised was gay, or 'homosexual', as we used to call it, and he said, 'Do I ever go to hotels or meet anybody?' and I said, 'No' and he said, 'Well, how about we go to a city hotel?' Now, bearing in mind in those years that everything in life was formal, I didn't know another gay person because of their dress or their manner – you knew it only by association.

Sex was also available in public parks and at beats, but Herbert was aware that 'people were starting to say they were bashed up in a park [or] in the street', as there were 'the laws of loitering with intent and therefore you could be caught by just not going into a toilet and [after using the facilities] coming straight out'.

When asked how he knew about the laws, Herbert replied: 'because I saw the police cars outside the toilets and policemen walking into the toilets'. 'Terrible things' happened to Herbert's friends who were caught soliciting.

Although Herbert had initially enjoyed sex at beats, his life was turned upside down one day when he was entrapped and charged:

> I picked this guy up and we went over to my car, got in, I noticed there was a police car up the hill a little bit, got in the car, and he said to me um, 'Sorry, mate, you're gone'. And ah, I said, 'What do you mean?' He said, 'I'm a policeman, I'm arresting you for loitering with intent'... They wanted a conviction so, therefore I thought, 'I'm not going to give it to them on a plate'. So, I said, 'I don't know what on earth you are talking about! I had to go to the toilet, yes, I did meet a nice guy, and I invited him to come home with me' [and] I said, 'That's it'.

He vividly recalled what happened immediately after:

> You were locked together with the females of the period, as almost the street walker, and therefore loitering with intent.

> And you were fingerprinted. You were taken, you were caught, you were fingerprinted, and you had to go to trial.

The charge threatened not only to end Herbert's career, but also to destroy his family relationships – particularly with his mother, who was unaware of his homosexuality. He:

> had the embarrassment of getting a good solicitor...so therefore in society it was not very pleasant for me, because ah, [people would ask] 'How did I get caught up in all this?' for example, because [for] all intents and purposes [in their minds] I'm straight.

Fortunately, Herbert knew a solicitor who worked in a well-known firm. He still faced the shame of explaining to a friend the lurid details of being picked up by the police. Later, a barrister advised him to plead guilty, which he did, and he was placed on a one-year good behaviour bond. This was a 'hideous' period in Herbert's life because he 'felt physically and mentally sick' with 'panic'. He could only think 'what a terrible situation I've got myself into'. What made things even more difficult was that he couldn't explain why he was 'picked up in the garden anyhow, in the toilet block', because 'why was I there at that time?! I couldn't associate it with my work!' He couldn't 'mention where [he was] working because that would be, make it even worse, 'cause it involves your professional life, it involves everything'. After this episode, Herbert found it very difficult to go to a public toilet even if he 'had too much to drink', because:

> you were now terribly aware, is there a policeman on our radar? It was control and awareness and putting panic into you...to the degree where it was hard to piddle.

Herbert believes that police were:

> trying to prove to a public that they were policing 'undesirables' – and homosexuals were 'undesirables'. We're no different to the rest of the world, but the word 'homosexual' was 'wrong', the act of homosexuality was 'deplorable'.

The other problem for Herbert was how to explain everything to his mother and the uncertainty around how she would react. After his father passed away, Herbert cared for his mother and lived with her in the same house, where life was 'pretty easy-going'. Because of his 'theatrical side', Herbert often had play readings at the house, and his mother would happily join in. He remembered:

> I would quite often come home to the house here and there would be Mum with a whole group of young people I knew that would say 'Hello Herbert' when I walked in the door... and I had met them, shall we say, in the gay life [and] we'd be much chuckling to each other, [as] unknown to Mum that that's how we knew each other!

But his arrest meant that 'suddenly that world of the beats [was] closed for people like me'. He also concluded that he had no choice but to reveal his homosexuality to his mother, because he knew a summons would arrive at the house:

> It was a double whammy for me. I had to tell Mum, and Mum interestingly enough, I thought would be easy with it, but in fact she performed exactly true to type of a loving mum. 'Oh, Herbert, how terrible!', crying her eyes out, and then she said, 'I've always been so worried that you kept changing friends, you never seemed to be able to keep your friends'. And then of course we discussed no children, and grandchildren, and that sort of thing, and not being married.

It was a very stressful period. It taught Herbert that homosexuals were fair game for police. If they wanted to survive, they needed to be constantly secretive about their activities. Yet, despite his suffering, Herbert's relationship with his mother actually improved once he had made his confession. He recalled that, on the same day he told his mother, her reaction:

> did have a funny side – if I could call it that. It would [have been]

about 3 or 4 o'clock in the morning, with all these horrible things happening, Mum made a comment, and she said, and she'd by then got out of bed, she said 'I think we can have some early breakfast, don't you?' So, Mum quickly as anything cooked some bacon and eggs, we sat down at the table and she said, 'Now, is Gerald gay?' 'Is *this* friend gay? Is *that* friend gay?' and then we started on film stars that we'd heard were homosexual! So, then we had an open discussion of it all [and] subsequently what we did do was... we turned the house into two flats. I lived on one side, Mum lived on the other side [and] we met for food. Even if I was 'entertaining', in inverted commas, they [homosexual friends] were coming home for dinner, Mum sneakily put some food into the stove on my side, and 'Oh, everything's cooked!!' So, I was very lucky, and Mum stonewalled anything of friends that might 'worry' about Herbert's *'friends'*.

Happily for Herbert, his mother became 'exceptionally, exceptionally' supportive of him 'right to the day she died and we managed to live a very happy life'. But, as Herbert came to realise, such maternal support was not only exceptional in postwar Australia – it was also unimaginable for most homosexual men.

Bernard and Robert's story

Treatment or prison: Bernard's story

Born in 1944, Bernard was 74 years old at the time of his interview. He lives in inner Melbourne with his long-term partner. He recalled becoming aware of his homosexuality 'probably when I was 10 or 12'. He grew up on an orchard property in country Victoria and travelled to both primary and secondary school on a bus, where he sat beside other boys and 'played games by putting our hands into each other's pockets'. Bernard understood that he was attracted to the boys and that he liked such games. He also enjoyed sexual contact with a boy from a dairy farm nearby. He particularly remembered a boy called Peter, with whom he would:

load up the family's utility with hay bales and go out into the paddocks and throw hay out to the cows, and then we'd sit in the back of the utility and jerk each other off!

This continued until the end of Bernard's secondary education and often spilled into school holiday activities – which Bernard thought 'was just marvellous!'

Bernard thought that, while the other boys 'just wanted to be jerked off', for him the sexual contact carried more meaning. Although he had read that 'this was just a phase that boys went through' (something that made him chuckle in his interview), he knew that it 'was different' for him, although he still expected that 'somehow it would all change' later. Because of his grandmother's influence, Bernard was brought up in a 'comfortable Presbyterian existence' – although he got his father's permission to stop attending Sunday School when he was 12, because, even at that age, he 'never felt a need for it'. He thought that the 'conservatism of the Church' in the 1950s was all 'pervasive [and] restrictive' and that; religion taught that the:

idea of pleasure almost was not to be desired, that life's fucking hard and should be hard and you deserve it, and if you don't deserve it now, you'll deserve to be belted later.

Bernard described postwar Australia as 'very conservative, especially in the country'. This became more of a reality for him when his:

older brother got a local girl pregnant. She was the daughter of a Catholic school teacher, [and] the priest got up in church and berated our family name.

In many ways, Bernard is thankful that his father countered this life view. Although his father had left school at 12, he was 'widely read' and a 'member of the Communist Party of Australia, [so there was] lots of Communist Party literature around the house'. His father was 'a battling, self-made man [who] always wanted to be independent'–

a quality Bernard still greatly admires. Bernard recalls this 'radical political background' to his childhood as being important to events that would soon define his very being. But his upbringing also instilled a strong sense of independence and freedom of thought in Bernard – qualities which later proved to be almost lifesaving for him as he faced immensely challenging issues at different stages.

After completing high school, Bernard relocated to Melbourne. He boarded with a friend at that person's grandmother's house and continued to have sex with him. After this period, he lived at the YMCA with the same boy with whom he had had sex in the utility. Here, he met 'lots of other boys', because 'there was a lot of activity' going on. Bernard laughed as he recalled that the YMCA had a swimming pool at the time; the rule stipulated that 'you had to swim in the nude!' He recalled: 'there was a lot of sex going on', not necessarily all homosexual sex – it was 'just horny young boys!'

Nevertheless, Bernard felt confused:

> I knew I was sexually attracted to men, but women were easier in terms of there were social things to go to, [such as] dances and things, and you know, I wasn't aware of beats or meeting men for sex in public places.

He had accessed some information from the International Bookshop, in Elizabeth Street Melbourne, which was 'run by the Communist Party and had lots of radical literature – not just about politics, it was about sex and everything else'. This made him aware that 'homosexuality [was] a criminal offence'. Unsurprisingly, Bernard felt at the time that he was 'leading a straight life [because] all my network was straight people'. At around 17, he had a girlfriend with whom 'for a couple of weeks we thought she was pregnant – [so] we'd clearly been fucking'.

But, around this time, an event took place that would impact Bernard's life for many years after. When he was 18, in 1962, he was 'picked up by the police in Richmond, on the Boulevard on the Yarra River, opposite *Leonda* restaurant' – which was a place where 'straight and gay people met in cars' to have sex. Bernard was caught with another 18 year-old male in the back seat of the car, both with their trousers around their ankles. The boys were separated. Both spent the night in jail and 'fronted the Magistrate's Court and subsequently the County Court', charged with 'gross indecency'. At the police station, the boys were forced to describe in detail what had occurred in the car and to separately sign confessions about their homosexual activities.

Those confessions and the court hearing that followed tell us much about the postwar era: attitudes to homosexuality, coercive policing techniques, the collusion between members of the law and medical fraternities and the general ignorance and prejudice that dictated the lives of so many homosexuals. Both confessions include details of a previous sexual encounter between the two boys and reveal the police's desire (perhaps even improper fascination) to extract as much intimate description as possible. In one section of the statement, Bernard writes:

> On the occassion (sic) about 2 to 3 weeks ago...we went to the Boulevard and stopped underneath the railway bridge...then we both took our trousers off...and we started to fondle each other's penis. While we were fondling, I put Robert's penis in my mouth and he put mine in his mouth. I can't remember whether I worked myself off or whether Robert did, but I ejected on the seat of the car. Shortly after that Robert drove me home to the flat and he left.

But the confessions also reveal a disturbing similarity of both structure and language, which indicates that the two (separated) boys were made to sign statements that in all likelihood were essentially produced by the police officers involved. It should be noted, too, that collusion between police may have occurred: Constable P. Buller took Bernard's statement and also witnessed Robert's statement.

Bernard recalled:

> The police, you know, I was grilled, and we were separated, and they got apologies, they got confessions out of us. I wasn't

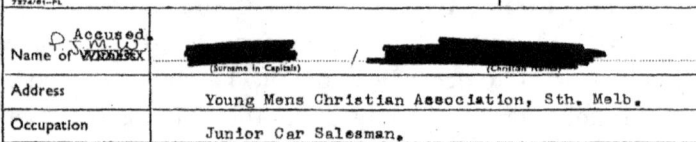

VICTORIA POLICE

STATEMENT

Form No. 287
Date 13/12/62

Name of Accused: [redacted]
Address: Young Mens Christian Association, Sth. Melb.
Occupation: Junior Car Salesman.

STATES—
I've known Terry KENNEDY for ten months or a year. I first met him at the Y.M.C.A. In about August, September, of this year, Terry left the Y.M.C.A. and went to live elsewhere. It would be two months ago when Terry called in at the Y.M.C.A. to see somebody there. I saw him in the lounge, we talked, and then I drove him home to his Flat. Terry invited me to call in to his Flat if I was ever out that way. One evening, possibly three weeks ago, I called in at the Flat to see if Terry, or some of the other boys he was living there with, had anything in the way of a meal. I saw Terry, and I had a meal there. We watched the Television for an hour or so, then I took Terry for a drive in my Car. We drove around the Sth. Eastern Freeway, and then took the road that runs alongside the river, we drove down this road and stopped under a Bridge, which I think was a Tram Bridge. We talked in general for a while, and then we both seemed to fondle one another. I took my trousers down, and Terry took his down also. During the time we were fondling one another I put Terry's penis in my mouth, and Terry put my penis into his mouth. I worked myself off and ejaculated over the back seat of the Car. Shortly after this I drove Terry home and I returned to the Y.M.C.A. Last night, that's Wednesday, I had some business to attend to off Malvern Road, and on my way back I called in to the Flat where Terry lives. There was another boy at the Flat with Terry. Terry and me had some beer, then we watched the mid-week movie on Television. After that I showed Terry a Fiat Car I had and he asked me if he could have a drive of it. He drove around in the Fiat and eventually we ended up under that Bridge where we were the last time. The Fiat Car has bucket seats fitted to it, we folded the back seat down and tipped the front bucket seats forward. Terry took his trousers down and lay down on the seat, I took my trousers down, and I lay on top him. My penis was errect and I was lying with my penis on Terry's stomach. We had'nt been laying like this for long when the Policeman flashed the torch inside the Car. I put my trousers back on and we went with the Policeman to the Police Station.
I did muck around when I was smaller with the next door neighbour. I gave it up when I got a bit older. I don't know what made me do what I did with Terry. I think I'm cured now, I'll be ruined for life if I don't stop now.

Statement taken and signature witnessed by me this 13th day of December 1962, at the Richmond Police Station in the presence of Constable BULLER.

(G. BRYANT) SNR/CONST. 11590.

(P.J. BULLER. CONST. 13645.)

Bernard's statement

	VICTORIA POLICE	Form No. 287
	STATEMENT	Date 13:12:62

Name of Accused	KENNEDY / Gordon James	
	(Surname in Capitals) (Christian Names)	
Address	11 Callantina Road, Hawthorn	
Occupation	Accountancy Student	

STATES— I met ▓▓▓▓▓ in about February or March of this year, at the Y.M.C.A. where we were both boarding, ▓▓▓ lived on the 4th floor and I lived on the 3rd. I shifted from the Y.M.C.A. in August this year and went to live at the flat in Hawthorn. I went to live at the flat with three other boys from the Y.M.C.A.

About a fortnight or 3 weeks ago, ▓▓▓ came to the flat to see if I could supply him with a meal as I had often gone in to the Y.M.C.A. to see my friends there, and on one of these visits I had asked him out to the flat if he was out that way. On one occasion I had gone to the Y.M.C.A., about 2 months previous, ▓▓▓ had driven me home. This was when I had invited him out again.

On the occasion about 2 to 3 weeks ago, I supplied ▓▓▓ with a meal and we had a fair bit of beer also. We then went and watched television for a while and then went for a drive in his car. We drove around in the car for a while and then went down to the Boulevard and stopped underneath the railway bridge which goes overhead. We then had a talk for a while and a smoke and then we both took our trousers off. After we took our trousers off we started to fondle each other's penis. Whilst we were fondling I put ▓▓▓ penis in my mouth and he put mine in his mouth. I can't remember whether I worked myself off, whether ▓▓▓ did, but I ejected on the seat of the car. Shortly after that ▓▓▓ drove me home to the flat and he left.

Last night (Wednesday), ▓▓▓ came to the flat at about 7 O'clock. I had a few drinks with ▓▓▓ and then we watched television, after I Had my evening meal. After my tea we watched the mid-week movie during which we had quite a lot to drink. After the movie finished I went for a drive with ▓▓▓ in his car. I drove around for a while and then we parked outside the flat. ▓▓▓ then took over the wheel and we went down to the Boulevard back to the same spot under the railway bridge where we went the first time. The car we were in was a Fiat and had bucket seats in the front which could be pushed forward, and the rear seat back was able to be folded down to make a bed. When we pulled up we both took our trousers off and I laid on the back seat, ▓▓▓ then laid on top of me. My penis was erect and was on my stomach, ▓▓▓ then began to work himself up against my stomach. It only seemed a matter of 2 or 3 minutes before the Policeman came and shone his torch inside the car. I then put my trousers on and we went with the Policeman to the Police Station.

I used to play with another boy's penis and he used to play with mine from about January 1961 to July 1961. I used to board with this boy at his ▓▓▓ relatives place in Oakleigh. I have never been to see a Psychiatrist or a Doctor about my abnormal behaviour.

I have read this statement and it is true & correct.

Gordon J. Kennedy.

Statement taken and signature witnessed by me this 13th day of December 1962, at the Richmond Police Station in the presence of Constable DOWDELL.

P.P.BULLER. Const 13645.

B.P.DOWDELL Const 14049.

Robert's statement

mindful of the fact of having any rights to call a solicitor, I was just terrorised by the whole thing.

Bernard was 'absolutely shattered' and had to confess to his (then divorced) father what had occurred, but he was also relieved that his father:

was fantastic, [and] not the least bit judgemental. He believed everybody had a life [and] all he wanted to do was look after his son.

Bernard knew that this response was 'unusual' for the era. It is only from a contemporary perspective that we can fully appreciate how extraordinary such support was at a time when many parents would have disowned their sons in the same situation, particularly given the lurid detail in the boys' confessions (reproduced here with permission from Bernard).

It is striking that both statements follow a similar narrative structure, suggesting that the separated boys were 'coached' in writing their confessions. Both documents begin with the boys' living arrangement histories; continue with the planned visit of Robert to

Structure	Bernard confession	Robert confession
Living arrangements history	met February or March this year	known for 10 months or a year
	met at YMCA	met at YMCA
	shifted from the YMCA in August this year	in about August, September of this year, left the YMCA
Planned visit	went to live at the flat	went to live elsewhere
	to see my friends	to see somebody
	if he was out that way	if I was ever out that way
	to supply him with a meal	in the way of a meal
	watched television for a while	watched the television for an hour or so

Defining 'homosexual': Legal, medical, and psychiatric interventions

Structure	Bernard confession	Robert confession
Planned drive	for a drive in my car	for a drive in his car
	stopped underneath the railway bridge	stopped under a bridge
	then had a talk for a while	we talked in general for a while
Description of sexual behaviour	then had a talk for a while we both took our trousers off	took my trousers down, and Bernard took his down also
	started to fondle each other's penis	seemed to fondle one other
	I put Robert's penis in my mouth	I put Bernard's penis in my mouth
	I can't remember whether I worked myself off	I worked myself off
	I ejected on the seat of the car	I ejaculated over the seat of the car
	shortly after that Robert drove me home	shortly after this I drove Bernard home
Establishing repeat behaviour	last night (Wednesday)	last night, that's Wednesday
	had a few drinks	had some beer
	watched the mid-week movie	watched the mid-week movie
	I drove around	he drove around in the Fiat
	bridge where we went the first time	bridge where we were the last time
	had bucket seats in the front	tipped the front bucket seats forward
	could be pushed forward	tipped the front bucket seats forward
	took our trousers off	Bernard took his trousers down ... I took my trousers down
	my penis was erect	my penis was erect

Structure	Bernard confession	Robert confession
Establishing repeat behaviour continued	laid on top of me	lay down on the seat
	was on my stomach	my penis on Bernard's stomach
	it only seemed a matter of 2 or 3 minutes	we hadn't been laying like this for long
Establishing correct police behaviour	the policeman came and shone his torch inside the car	the policeman flashed his torch inside the car
	I then put my trousers on	I put my trousers back on
	and we went with the policeman to the Police Station	and we went with the policeman to the Police Station
History of behaviour 3rd time	I used to play with another boy's penis	I did muck around when I was smaller with the next-door neighbour
Admission of guilt and knowledge of wrong-doing	I have never been to a psychiatrist or doctor about my abnormal behaviour	I think I'm cured now, I'll be ruined for life if I don't stop now

Bernard's home; describe a planned drive together; describe their sexual behaviour while in the car together; establish such behaviour as having taken place before; attest to 'correct' police procedure having been followed; offer a history of such sexual behaviour originating from childhood; and finally, admit guilt and knowledge of wrongdoing – all leading to a guilty confession.

Even more compelling evidence of police collusion is shown by a language analysis. The table above lists 35 separate words or phrases that either exactly match or are similar in content. Phrases such as 'I put Robert's penis in my mouth', 'I worked myself off', 'I ejected', 'I ejaculated' and 'my penis was erect' are notable in that, purportedly, both boys separately used such mirroring language. The 'guilt' of both boys is firmly established by the inclusion at the end of each statement that their behaviour was 'abnormal', required psychiatric intervention and could be 'cured'.

Further circumstantial evidence that the police authored much of what is included in the statements is the register of the language used. Whereas 18-year-old boys would conceivably use vernacular, such as 'I sucked him', 'I had an erection', or 'I came on the seat of the car', the statements instead use a formal, distancing language: 'I put my penis in his mouth', 'my penis was erect', and 'I ejected on the seat of the car'. It also seems implausible that 18 year olds with little sexual knowledge at the beginning of the 1960s would have alone concluded that they needed to see a psychiatrist about 'abnormal behaviour' or that they would reach the conclusion that they would be 'ruined for life' if they continued their homosexual activities.

At the urging of a solicitor, Bernard and his father engaged 'a barrister in William Street [Melbourne]' who would 'be supportive'. The barrister's name was John Hedigan. He later became a judge of the Supreme Court of Victoria and was described as a 'fiercely

Yarra Boulevard in Richmond provided some privacy for intimacy

independent individual in mind and spirit and a fearless advocate'.⁹ On Thursday 1 August 1963, 'the prisoners' (as listed on the court documents) Bernard and Robert appeared in the 'Melbourne Court of General Sessions before his Honor (sic) Judge Cussen' on two counts of 'committing [an] act of gross indecency'. Both accused pleaded guilty.

In his opening remarks, Mr Hedigan outlines that Bernard's parents 'divorced when he was 13', that he 'has a number of brothers and sisters', that he is now 'employed by a Chartered accountant and is doing an accountancy course', that he 'was living in a flat at the time this offence [sic] occurred but has returned home to live with his father and brother', and that 'he plays tennis and attends football matches'. The judge then inquires whether his parents are 'people of good repute?' He is informed that Bernard's 'father knows about this trouble' and will be called as a witness. Mr Hedigan also notes that: 'for the last couple of months the lad has been associated regularly with a young woman' – in all likelihood to present a sense of 'normality' and heterosexuality in Bernard's character. The barrister then calls Dr Guy Hale Springthorpe, a psychiatrist Bernard's father had engaged to argue that Bernard was 'getting treatment' for his homosexual tendencies. Although the psychiatrist's evidence is shocking from a contemporary perspective, Bernard felt that he was actually 'supportive'. In retrospect, Bernard believed that it was the evidence of Dr Springthorpe that boosted his case for clemency, recalling that the psychiatrist:

> was very good. He gave me all the Jacques [Lacan's psychological] tests and all that stuff and I didn't feel he was judging me. He knew he had a young guy who was now going to be jailed if he didn't [help]. I think he may have in fact told the judge that 'cause he's had sex with women he'll probably end up being a heterosexual.

Further, Bernard now thinks that Dr Springthorpe 'knew that I was going to be gay, but he thought it was an unjust crime'. Even if Dr Springthorpe had been sympathetic, his line of argument and evidence provide a stark insight into the way in which both the law and medicine could criminalise and pathologise homosexuality for their own ends in postwar Australia. In his opening address to the court, Dr Springthorpe notes Bernard's recent 'manifestations of this disorder' in his homosexual behaviour. He also informs the judge that 'as far as I can find out none of [Bernard's brothers and sisters] have homosexual tendencies' – indicating that he has already conducted investigations into the sexual preferences of Bernard's siblings! In contemporary times, we would consider such action a gross breach of privacy. The doctor continues by noting the 'not infrequent homosexual phase that adolescent boys go through'. In Bernard's case, he thought: 'that I should first try to assess the type and degree of the homosexual deviation'. He stressed that 'I do not think [Bernard] is the type of person who has a predeliction (sic) for young boys now that he is getting older', thus conflating the issues of homosexuality and paedophilia, as was common during the era. Language such as 'disorder' and 'deviation' points to mental illness and abnormality – because it was not heterosexual behaviour.

Dr Springthorpe adds to his psychological assessment summary by stating that Bernard's 'main activities have been with people of his own age group' and that 'this is important from the point of view of how he is to be handled and if he is a risk to the community'. The use of 'risk' highlights the danger homosexuals were believed to pose to society. The doctor continues: 'I could not get any evidence that [Bernard] has actually committed buggery' and that Bernard is 'of reasonable character and...not mentally defective'. Laws against buggery date from 1533 in Britain, where it was described in the courts as a 'detestable and abominable vice'.[10] It is a particularly emotive word. It carries the meaning of anal intercourse, as well as the stigma of acts against nature and God. The doctor's argument also gives insight into the role of women in postwar society as a marker of 'normality' in men: he tells the judge that Bernard has 'recently...been going out with a young lady on a rather more purposeful basis', but that 'he had not had sexual relations with the opposite sex'. Given that Bernard was still only 18 and unmarried at the time of the court appearance, it would seem (supposedly) problematic for him to have been able to have such relations at the time anyway, because sex outside of marriage was condemned in postwar Australia.

The judge asks the doctor to outline the 'sort of treatment' he recommends, to which he replies:

> The first is a general one of the supervisory nature, where one would attempt to encourage him along social lines, by which he would develop heterosexual behaviour normally, leaving things to nature. If that were not successful, there would be involved psychiatric treatment extending over years.

He continues by stating:

> Having regard to his youth, and the fact that he has some heterosexual tendencies, the degree of deviation is not as wide as one sometimes sees, and I think there is a likelihood that he can be helped. The fact that people say that they want to give up these practices is a demonstration of their motivation, which is an important step.

Clearly, the judge believes homosexuality to be a crime and a mental illness, and the psychiatrist contends that it is 'treatable', given a cooperative attitude from the 'patient'.

Judge Cussen then informs the two prisoners that they:

> could be sent to jail for three years for this, but I think I will give you an opportunity this time, but I will promise you this, that if you break the bond that I will give you, you will most certainly go to jail for 18 months, do you understand that?

Bernard was placed on a bond with the stipulation that he 'communicate with you, doctor (sic), or any person that you will nominate'. He was also fined £50, (the equivalent of $1,479 in 2020), or approximately 35 days' wages for a skilled tradesman at the time.[11]

Unsurprisingly, the whole experience was traumatic for Bernard and affected other important decisions he made during his life.

Bernard recalled the judge as 'dreadful' and understood that he:

> was absolutely looking forward to sending these 'two boys' he described to jail for three months, just to let them know what happens if you had sex with other males.

Bernard fully understood that the judge's opinion of homosexuals was 'quite fixed, as was indeed the police'.

The trauma continued even after the confessions had been signed, because Bernard:

> actually ended up in the divvy van to go to Pentridge because my bail money hadn't arrived. Fifty quid fine and someone was trying to find it, but it didn't come, and I'm actually in a divvy van at Richmond Police Station with the door slammed shut, looking at the other men around me thinking, 'What the fuck is going on here!?' They started the vehicle to back out, then they turned it off, the door opened, [and they said] 'Brown, your money's arrived'. I mean people have got no idea what that's like. That was a thing which I'll never forget.

The impact of his arrest has left Bernard with a lasting horror of authority in the form of the police:

> the power which they still have is something that terrifies me. I was just a boy who'd come down from the country a couple of years earlier, living in a flat with some other boys and having these affairs on Wednesday night. But it was the fact of experiencing that [the arrest and court case] and not wanting to experience it again.

Now aged 74, Bernard still feels the emotions of that time deeply, recalling:

> it hurt me so much. I'd suffered so much pain by, by having a gay experience that that just overwhelmed me, that I didn't want to go back there.

He believes that 'had the police not stopped, not picked me up, I would have just evolved, into a gay life'. Instead, he 'lived a hidden life for those 14 or 15 years' and:

> didn't touch another male from the age of 17 or 18 until I was 30 or 31 due to fear! Just having gone through the bloody experience of being charged [and] going to court, and it being illegal too, of course.

Like many other homosexual men from the era, Bernard struggled to reconcile his homosexual desire with the cultural and intellectual challenges of reimagining something that was so reviled. He summarised his experience of the law by observing: 'if anything was going to put you off homosexuality, that was'.

Viewing homosexual history through a blunt heterosexual/homosexual binary risks missing nuances that can reveal hidden histories. Bernard's story illustrates this complexity. Despite his attraction to men, he found women easier to socialise with. He 'value[d] family and children' and 'because I could engage in heterosexual activity and relate to women...I didn't feel any great deprivation'. On reflection, Bernard is certain that his earlier trauma influenced his decision to marry at age 28. In his words, 'it was enough to keep me straight!'. He also felt, at the time, that 'the straight life was a simpler life'. Consequently, he married a much younger woman because 'we were in love and we had a good relationship'. Nevertheless, Bernard was aware that he was suppressing homosexual feelings. Plans to start a family didn't eventuate. Two years later, Bernard's wife told him that she was leaving the marriage to be with one of his work colleagues.

After his wife left him, Bernard began a relationship with another woman, with whom he 'bonded both mentally and physically'. Even so, although this relationship involved a lot of sex, he didn't feel sexually satisfied. Perhaps his partner felt the same, because she returned from an overseas trip and announced that she had met someone else. Bernard was 'devastated' and asked, 'Where does this leave me?' At the age of 30, Bernard thought: 'Christ, I've got to resolve this' and 'made the decision to come out' and to fully acknowledge his homosexuality. He began 'looking at books and looking at reference texts or talking to people and getting [information] through them. Today you [just] Google it!' He explained: 'I advertised in *The Nation Review* that I wanted to meet people and get in step with the gay world' and consequently had his first gay 'hook-up'. Later, Bernard found a gay friendly hotel in Carlton (Melbourne) and:

> started meeting and picking up people, and I thought 'Oh, fuck! This is glorious! How long has this been around for?!' [From then on] I was homosexual, and you know, let's get into it!

When asked if this made him happier, Bernard had no hesitation in responding:

> Oh, yes! Yes! Happier, yes. In fact, it was interesting, looking back I used to suffer a lot from sweating, you know – physical sweating, the arms and stuff, and also a few allergies and things, and I think they were all connected with the unresolved sexual issue. And they suddenly all went away. Not suddenly, but over a period.

But, after his first same-sex relationship ended, Bernard became depressed. He decided to see a psychiatrist to help him to 'recognise things that I can resolve that are resolvable [and] things that I have to accept'. He initially received some counselling from a friend who was studying psychiatry, but the friend 'hadn't finished his exams', so he suggested that Bernard consult someone fully qualified. He advised Bernard that:

> there are two sorts [of psychiatrists] you can go to – you can go to someone who's a supportive type and will say 'There, there, it will all work', or you can have somebody who's quite direct. I said 'I'll have the direct one, thank you!'

In the end he 'saw a guy called Bill Orchard' who was 'very supportive in [that] I never felt he was judging one way or the other'.

The psychiatrist 'specialised in group therapy' and initially gave Bernard 'a book to take home and read'. In the end, Bernard did '15 years of psychotherapy and [his] depression went pretty quickly'. The whole process was 'fascinating' and 'very valuable' for him.

Almost 60 years after Bernard's harrowing experience with the law, a further momentous event needs to be included in his story. In the years following his 'coming out', Bernard 'got involved in gay politics and worked towards law reform', particularly through the Homosexual Law Reform Coalition. He recalled that, during the period (1970s–1990s):

> we used to go out on speaking engagements, you know, we'd go to Geelong [Victoria's second largest city] and talk to Rotary or we'd go to Ballarat [Victoria's third largest city] or somewhere – and talk to society groups. I'd stand up and say, 'Look, you know, I'm just like you! It's just that I prefer to go to bed with a man – you prefer to go to bed with women but, you know, I go to the races, I don't smoke, but I have a bet, I have an occasional drink. I'm just a bloke who likes men'.

Even Bernard's friends who 'had known me for 20 years as a straight person' were 'all confronted, saying "Well, what can we do?"', to which he would reply: 'Well, it's up to you – I'm still me!'. Yet, although Bernard worked hard to accept his homosexuality and to live a more open and satisfying life, he acknowledged that his earlier conviction still 'haunted' him. It remained as a criminal record. Fittingly, Bernard was one of four men invited to be present in parliament when the Victorian Government apologised to gay men in 2016. His criminal record had been expunged – although even this was a very emotionally confronting process:

> all my criminal records [that appear in this chapter] had to be dug up [by the] Justice Department...and the woman [who did so] warned me, 'You may find some of this threatening'.

Not until then had the full emotional impact of how close he came to imprisonment become apparent to Bernard.

Medicine and psychiatry

In seeking to understand and interpret the stories of interviewees about their experience of general practice doctors and psychiatrists in postwar Australia, I next examine who those medical practitioners were and the social milieu they came from. It is probable that postwar medical practitioners had done their training in the early part of the 20th century. Most would have been educated from around 1900 to the 1930s. Comparatively very few of them were women, because entry to the medical fraternity was controlled by a male-dominated institution that protected its own privilege. Medical degrees were costly and lengthy, and men were usually supported by wealthy families. They therefore enjoyed personal autonomy and social power and were more likely to be socially conservative.[12]

It is also important to record that the elevated role and professional and social position of doctors and psychiatrists in the postwar era was firmly entrenched. Now, it is not unusual for patients to ask questions about a doctor's diagnosis or treatment – even to seek a second opinion. In the 1940s and 1950s, a doctor's authority was more universally absolute. His (or her) opinion was not commonly challenged. Ryan, 76, who later became a doctor himself, illustrated just how much power doctors held. He recalled:

> when I was in about fourth year high school, I was very worried because I noticed that there were, I had little yellow spots on my scrotum and I remember um, saying to my mother, 'I think I need to go and see the doctor...because I've got something', and the interesting thing is I didn't say it to my father because my relationship with my dad was never really good, not to talk about something personal, you know...So I rang up and made an appointment and I went to see him, and he was a very bluff, rough, you know, typical sort of old GP...and I said to him, 'I've got these yellow spots'. 'Well', he said, 'let's have a look', and so he had a look and he said 'Oh, it's nothing to worry about!' he

said, 'absolutely nothing to worry about!'. He said 'you shouldn't be worried about stuff like that!' and, and with no explanation no, no telling me what they were! Nothing! You know! I thought, I mean imagine going and talking to him about something that was really important!!

Homosexuality was clearly an unmentionable topic. The *Textbook of Medical Treatment* (first published in 1938) for example, declares in a chapter on 'Psychiatry in General Practice':

> To the patient the doctor is necessarily someone of great prestige and wisdom, possessed of the secrets of life and death, and when the patient approaches him (sic) he is usually afraid and bewildered and sometimes guilty...He should recognise the patient who resembles the anxious insecure child who clings to the parent for support and refuses to grow up.[13]

World War II had spiked interest in psychological disturbances and the way people dealt with anxiety and the frustrations of living. Sigmund Freud's (1856–1939) development of psychoanalysis had become highly influential in the diagnosis and treatment of mental illnesses, which included homosexuality.[14] Yet, postwar medical manuals provided little insight into the 'condition'. Dunlop, Alstead and Macgregor write in 1968 (a decade after the postwar era!) that 'sexual maladjustments':

> seen by the practitioner are of a kind in which his [Freud's] therapy is likely to be effective. There are others, however, which require lengthy investigative techniques if, indeed, they can be treated at all...it is for the practitioner to...support [the homosexual] in coming to an adjustment which will enable him to avoid anti-social activity. Homosexuals are, however, more prone to suffer from neurosis than those with normal sexual attitudes, and these patients should be referred to the psychiatrist.[15]

We can only surmise what the authors meant by 'anti-social

activity', but they were possibly referring to homosexual men seeking and participating in homosexual sex. The invisibility of the subject is evident, possibly illustrated by this one single paragraph in a book with 750 pages. Clearly, homosexual sex is not seen as 'normal', and those who indulge are considered more likely to suffer from mental illness.

In 1948, Noyes and Kolb wrote about 'the homosexual' in their chapter on 'Paranoia and Paranoid Conditions'. They concluded that it was probably caused by a mother fixation and that boys transfer their sexual energy to the people who attract their mothers, that is men.[16] A decade and a half later, medical opinion on homosexuality had not changed. Writing in the *South African Journal of Science* in May 1962, Renée Liddicoat notes: 'one of the fields of abnormal behaviour most neglected by research workers is homosexuality'.[17]

In 1940s and 1950s Australia, and even well into the 1960s and early 1970s, the medical world responded to homosexuality with either silence or treatment. Doctors and psychiatrists were sometimes complicit in assisting the law to be applied in brutal ways. Silence was imposed through a lack of scientific or cultural information about homosexuality in medical knowledge and publications and a societal aversion to mentioning the topic. Homosexuals feared discussing the topic with their doctors because a declaration of aberrant sexuality could lead to a humiliating prognosis, psychological treatment or – worse – being reported to the police. There was little reason to confide in anyone in the medical world. Of the 27 men in this book, only two mentioned ever revealing their homosexuality to a doctor or psychiatrist – and one had little choice, being involved with the law. Those who mentioned doctors explained that dialogue with them simply would not have happened because of prevailing attitudes to homosexuality. Shockingly, these men did not feel empowered to seek any assistance or knowledge from doctors about their homosexuality until the 1980s – decades after the postwar era.

Analysing deviancy

Staying mum: Arthur's story
Asked whether he had ever discussed his homosexuality with a medical person, Arthur, 74, replied: 'I never actually mentioned it to doctors, no, no...[because] I didn't think it was, possibly, well, I wasn't that upset about it'. He recalled that, despite:

> the problems that I might have had in my early teens, I seemed to get over it all...[by] just accepting life, accepting that you know there were certain laws and limitations that you just had to fit in with.

I also asked Arthur what he thought would have happened if he had gone to a doctor in the 1950s and declared himself as homosexual. His answer was instructive:

> Oh, I'd hate to imagine – they'd probably say that you need some sort of treatment. Well, certainly the doctor that I went with, like the family doctor, I, I couldn't imagine him being particularly liberated and I'd certainly only see him if ah, if you were really, you know sick, whether it was just the flu or...Fortunately, I never had any major problems with health, but, so, it would have been just very minor, but I certainly wouldn't, I certainly wouldn't have liked Dr Gill, I don't think I would have liked to of, brought up the topic with him.

Arthur's response points to the self-imposed silence by homosexuals about their sexuality when seeing a doctor and to the reasons. Most homosexuals felt uncomfortable revealing themselves until decades later. Even if doctors and psychiatrists at the time had accepted homosexuality (and there is scant evidence that they did), the unwillingness of homosexuals to place themselves in danger also hampered progress in the medical world's education about them.

Waves: Rory's story
Eighty-year-old Rory's story took place when he was in his early 30s, at

the beginning of the 1970s. Although that is outside the era this book covers, it is worth noting, precisely because it illustrates just how much contemporary psychiatry has shifted its view of homosexuality. This shift did not even begin to emerge until at least two decades after the postwar era. Rory sought medical help by visiting his GP, where he revealed his homosexuality and said that he was 'worried about it'. But he found little support. Rory recalled the visit because he was:

> pretty sure he [the doctor] was a Catholic, so he wasn't much help. He just said, well, he'd send me to a psychiatrist, and again, the first psychiatrist he mentioned wasn't a Christian – he was Jewish, so I said...I wanted to see a Christian psychiatrist. (Oh, dear, look, this is just so embarrassing!) So, I was sent to a Christian psychiatrist...[and] his theory was to lie on the beach and listen to the waves!! And I thought, 'Well, that's bloody useless!'

Unsurprisingly, Rory did not then fully acknowledge his homosexuality until he was around 40. He was unable to form a relationship with another man until he was 68. He has a deep sense of loss that he 'didn't have a relationship, or couldn't start a relationship, say, in my 20s'. And his great regret is 'not being able to be who I am – that I feel for most of my life that I've pretended to be somebody else'.

Defining 'homosexual'

In 1953, Harvey Sutton from the 'Father and Son Welfare Movement' wrote in the *Sydney Morning Herald* that homosexuality was not 'congenital' but rather developed in early life. He concluded that a positive outcome of this new knowledge was that it 'has made possible an entirely new approach to the problem, its treatment and means of prevention'.[18] His opinion neatly summarises the postwar medicalised approach to the meanings of homosexuality. It is an affliction on society, an illness that requires a cure, and its practice needs to be repressed by legal, medical or other means. Homosexuality, homosexual sex, homosexual culture and homosexual identity were defined by legislators, police, lawyers, doctors, psychiatrists and people in positions of power – rarely by homosexuals themselves, other than in private and guarded settings. It is little wonder that it remained hidden, secret, shameful and generally unspoken. It is even less surprising that most homosexuals spent their lives finding ways to survive without revealing their deeply concealed same-sex attraction.

Postwar Australian laws purportedly safeguarded all citizens. In practice, they privileged heterosexual citizens, because homosexuality forfeited the right to protection by the state. Social institutions such as the law, medicine and religion held virtually unchallenged authority, and the impacts of their dogmas extended deep into the lives of those who transgressed. They often worked together against aberrant sexuality to achieve the shared objective of imprisoning the homosexual, both figuratively and literally. Patriarchal power controlled the lives of women and homosexual men in different ways. To be defined as homosexual signalled first and foremost buggery. It had ramifications for a man's employment, family relations, friendships, religious beliefs, education, social life, topics of permissible discussion, what he revealed about himself, how he walked and held himself, the way he sat, the way he stood, what pastimes he liked or pretended to like, where he went, to whom he spoke and, most importantly, to whom (if anyone) he revealed his true self. Most (although not all) homosexuals lacked agency to define 'homosexual' or to freely shape their own lives. How that struggle manifested in their lives is explored in the following chapters.

3

Constructing 'homosexual': Integration of self

The enigma of difference

How does one 'become' homosexual? Becoming an artist, or a doctor, a comedian or simply a good raconteur requires development of knowledge, skill and solid practice. 'Becoming' something implies a process one can follow, with aims and objectives guiding the pathway to achievement. For men in 1940s and 1950s Australia, 'becoming' homosexual had none of those advantages, because the outcome was not only shameful and disparaged; its practice was also illegal. How could boys who were taught nothing of the topic – its experiences, emotions, desires, practices and meanings – even begin to learn about who they were? More particularly, how could they even begin to comprehend the impact homosexuality would have on their sexual experiences, their cultural understanding and the choices they would make about how they constructed their lives? How did they manage to survive without knowledge of the part of themselves that would impact so much on their life experience?

Crucial to their stories was how these men came to understand their 'difference' and how they connected that difference with their sexuality. For some, it was a pragmatic and relatively swift process. For most, it involved an extended period (sometimes decades) of self-doubt and confusion. Colin, 80, declared: 'I knew I was different, but I had no idea what it was'. This understanding arrived in varying ways and influenced life outcomes differently. Realisation of difference was a starting point: recognising that socially 'normal' ideas of masculinity and heterosexuality did not sit comfortably with many. They had a troubling sense that they could not live up to these expectations. The movement towards the naming of their sexuality typically progressed without much insight into what exactly their 'failings' were and why they were viewed so critically.

This struggle for clarity was particularly evident while the men were still young schoolboys, effectively searching for answers without even knowing the questions. From primary school through the early and middle years of secondary school, most were particularly aware of their difference and especially attuned to other boys who lacked sporting prowess or an interest in sport. Not showing an interest in girls during their teenage years was also an indication of difference from other boys. Actively pursuing sport and girls demonstrated masculinity; not doing so aroused suspicion and gave permission to others to launch personal attacks. Not living up to these expectations profoundly impacted lives. A man's character was then connected to 'effeminacy' and, by extension, homosexuality – even if that notion was still largely undefined.

A significant minority of men did manage to navigate these challenges without undue concern about their sexuality or their place within their own social world. The factors that allowed those boys to avoid the emotional and psychological distress are an important part of this history. Further, while the majority faced enormous challenges in 'becoming homosexual', there were also important differences in their experiences. Some boys understood their difference but were unable to disguise it – paying a high price for their 'flaw'. A second group did not have any awareness of their homosexuality as boys, and other students too failed to notice any difference. The third and largest group involved boys who realised their difference but were able to 'pass' and avoid negative consequences – often at great cost to their self-confidence and enjoyment of life.

This largest group of men continued 'passing' once they reached adulthood. They remained constantly vigilant about how they presented, to whom they talked, the subjects they broached and the places they frequented. Others were able to live relatively free and happy (homosexual) lives. These men lived within boundaries imposed by heterosexual society, particularly when they were not in homosexual settings, yet found ways to subvert cultural and legal rules. Condemnatory language held fewer fears for them. Although living a fully open homosexual life was not possible, they enjoyed more comfortable lives than those whose struggle was more intense. Remarkably, all the men in this book found ways to survive their challenges in their search for what a homosexual life could mean.

Early years: navigating school, sport, effeminacy and compulsory heterosexuality

Compounding their lack of knowledge about homosexuality, these men had no older adult role models to offer knowledge, advice or nurturing. The contradiction between the public self and the private homosexual self was therefore confusing, stressful, threatening – but unspoken. It was linked to seemingly abstract ideas about demonstrations of masculinity through sporting ability, social interests and ways of physically presenting oneself. Nelson and Martin refer to some of the literature of the time which provided theories of how a boy could become a man. They quote US sex expert Patricia Campbell as believing that: 'a man's sexual character was both the model and the source for the rest of his character'.[1] To fail the test of 'normal' heterosexual masculinity, therefore, could only mean the opposite – a feminised misrepresentation of manhood that invited ridicule. Boys perceived as feminine or homosexual, or both, provided a contrast to enable heterosexual boys to build their own masculine identity. When referring to his own lack of knowledge about homosexuality and the complete absence of reference to it, Nigel, 74, remarked on the lack of information, but: 'Where was the information to go?!' His confusion lasted for 'around 10 to 15 years' while he was 'in denial' because 'I felt that I was not that [effeminate] stereotype'. Nigel consequently became 'withdrawn' and felt a deep regret for the loss of 'the best years of my life'.

As boys, most struggled to understand that their difference related to same-sex attraction. They were more likely to simply connect it with something sinful and deviant. A preference for academic pursuits and a lack of sporting prowess and of interest in prescribed 'masculine' activities invited unwelcome labels such as 'sissy' and brought shame to the boy and his family. At school, other students and, occasionally, teachers made such connections clear through bullying behaviour, name calling, physical intimidation and exclusion. This (perceived) failing in the performance of masculinity energised other boys and male adults to exercise 'authority and social power' over their victims. Many of the boys did not have the interest or ability to even feign sporting prowess. The enduring trauma of this bullying – their faltering voices, their need for silent reflection and their shifting body language – was evident 60, 70, or 80 years after the incidents.

Realising and not passing

The confusion of not belonging: Spencer's story
Boys' experiences at school (and later as adults in the workforce) varied according to their ability to 'pass' as heterosexual. The way a boy was expected to conduct himself at school was very often determined by the influence of sport. Other boys, teachers and parents expected that males should be not only interested in sport but preferably skilled at it. Those unable to demonstrate this had doubts raised about the authenticity of their masculinity. Spencer, 74, for example, recalled:

> at school I felt a bit of an outcast because I...was never interested in sport. That was quite a strong concern for me, and it meant...that I was very bad at school and couldn't be bothered and failed all left, right and centre.

Spencer's lack of sporting prowess fed into perceptions that he did not belong in the group, and this affected his desire to achieve academically. By the time he was 16, Spencer was aware that he was not acting in the same way as other boys.

> I was starting to realise that everyone else had girlfriends and I
> started to do that, and I couldn't work out why I wasn't attracted
> to girls, or not so much even attracted – just, I just couldn't get
> it together.

There was no explanation for his difference. Without any real physical or emotional urge to do so, he attempted to mirror the behaviour of his classmates, creating a void in his sense of self and puzzlement about what was expected of him. Unaware of homosexual possibilities, he found no alternative to the heterosexual model being presented to him.

The price of disclosure: Paul's story
Paul, 76, had an even harder time at school because he inadvertently revealed his same-sex desire to his classmates. He has been punished ever since. He described a pivotal event that had a lasting, painful impact on him:

> My parents used to go to the local cinema on a Friday night and
> a boy called Keith, over the road, had a deal with my sister that
> he'd come over and show her his erect cock and she was to
> show him her private parts. Keith was old enough to have a
> really good cock!

Unfortunately, Paul 'opened [his] big mouth at school' about his delight in looking at male genitalia and 'life was hell from then on'. He experienced physical abuse by other boys. He recalled: 'you'd be playing football and all of a sudden you'd be slammed', highlighting the way in which violence was perpetrated under the guise of sport. By the time he was 12, Paul had begun to understand that same-sex attraction was deviant. When Keith's brother asked Paul to kiss him, Paul's response was 'NO! no! no! no! no! no!' A connection between homosexual expression and unnaturalness began to form in his mind. This learning was reinforced by religion, because Paul recalled:

> by then I was aware, I was brought up in a Baptist household, and

> I was aware of sin and not being the done thing for boys to do.

This seemed to clarify his growing sense of what he really wanted:

> I was really attracted to Keith and I wasn't interested in his brother and so then I realised that there is something going on – there is a deep attraction which wasn't reciprocated.

Vague possibilities of homosexuality seemed to be overwhelming Paul, but making sense of his feelings was still perplexingly challenging. He could only conclude that: 'maybe I was a bit of a cuckoo'. His family also considered him an 'oddball' because he liked reading and art, despite there being 'just one artwork…in the house'. When he started art school, 'they used to tease me about being the "mad artist" – don't you dare cut off your ear!' Somehow, an interest in the arts connected with homosexuality, which then also linked with mental illness – albeit in a nebulous, ill-defined way.

Paul's experience illustrates how an undefined but transgressive label of perceived homosexuality could be weaponised against any boy who was marked as different. Often, the cover of sporting violence concealed attacks. Powerful, masculine heterosexuality was strongly connected to sporting ability. A 1959 manual, *Instructions for boys*, advises 'a keenness for adventure and the desire to excel at manly sports' as a pathway to the type of man society expected a boy to become.[2] A lack of such qualities indicated a bent towards the non-masculine or the feminine – further confirmed by interest in academic development or a preference for literature, music and the arts. Whether or not a boy's mannerisms were effeminate didn't really matter; if he was 'different', other students *interpreted* them as effeminate.

A bitter label: Ryan's story

The idea of normative masculinities was thus introduced very early into a schoolboy's psyche. How could those who did not naturally possess 'masculine' traits 'become' what was expected of them? Ryan's emerging realisation of difference illustrates the experience of disconnect around not being a 'real' boy/man. He was 76 at the time of his interview. Born and raised in country New South Wales, Ryan explained that, at the age of seven:

> I knew I was attracted to a boy at school...he was the brother of a boy in my class, two years ahead of us at school and I thought he was wonderful!

He added: 'I wouldn't say that I knew I was gay then, [but] I realised I was attracted to boys'. By 13 or 14, he understood his attraction to mean that he was homosexual. Despite this awareness, Ryan faced enormous challenges in coming to understand this sexuality. Fitting this knowledge into his life was difficult, because he was:

> brought up in a very religious house. We were Baptists. So, there were lots of things we didn't do. Like, we didn't go to the movies, and we didn't swear, and we didn't smoke, and we didn't drink and so, you didn't tell dirty stories, didn't associate with 'rough' boys.

There was already an expectation within his family that Ryan had to maintain a 'correct' standard of male behaviour and reject much of what were considered 'normal' male adolescent characteristics. But what did 'normal' mean? His family expected him to be a refined, well-mannered, learned and, above all, pious boy. At school, the other boys expected him to be sporty, rough, uninterested in scholarship and not particularly cooperative with teachers. These restrictions on 'how' he could develop only added to the difficulties he faced in trying to fit in at school. Which masculinity should he emulate? And what would be the consequences of aiming for one over the other?

What came next for Ryan revealed some of the answers. By the early years of high school, his family had moved to Sydney, where Ryan attended a boys' high school 'which was a bit of a sporty school'. Unfortunately for Ryan, he 'had a bad time' outside classes because he was bullied:

> I was no good at sport, and I guess I was a bit of a 'sissy' basically

> and I suppose I didn't have the social skills to try and pretend that I wasn't what I was and that you know, I liked things like reading and artistic sort of stuff, and I was always good at school work and I didn't try to pretend I wasn't, so that I think that was because, I don't know if it's the same now, but in those times there was like this feeling that you know, you were a 'goody-goody' if you were. And I suppose it was those sorts of things that made me appear to be different.

Ryan reiterated that sport 'was a very important thing to be good at'. A lack of sporting ability was directly connected to effeminacy, through language that sought to feminise and expressed disapproval of skills or characteristics that other boys did not value. This intertwining of language and sporting culture worked to separate and silence any possibility that homosexuality and sporting prowess could be an alternative normative masculinity, even when both were evident. Another interviewee, Harold, provided a clear example of the power of this narrative to demonise. He was 75 at the time of his interview, but lessons learned as a young boy still lingered:

> It was pretty well-known for example, in the sporting world that there were a number of sporting heroes [in the AFL (Australian Football League)] that were 'poofters' and you know, that was something that had to be kept quiet. I don't think anybody had a reason to touch [discuss] it.

This process of enforced heterosexualisation and masculinisation began very early at school through the actions and discourse of the school community. The boys soon discovered that any deviation from these arrangements marked them out as 'different'. Other important adult figures, including mothers, fathers, brothers and teachers, often condoned such labelling. Terms such as 'sissy' conveyed meanings of femininity and weakness. 'Difference' was obliquely connected to sexual deviancy – even if the term 'homosexual' was not part of other boys' vocabulary. Ryan's natural inclinations towards the arts, his lack of sporting ability and his interest in study made him 'appear to be different' and connected him to being feminine. Consequently, the other boys gave Ryan a female name:

> My sister... who was three years younger, was called 'Rosamond' and the boys used to hear me talking to her and calling her 'Rosie' and they must have thought it was 'Rose' and they then started calling me 'Rose'.

This became 'uncomfortable and embarrassing and hurtful' – particularly 'if I was out walking with my family and some kid from school would shout out "Hi, Rose!"'. Ryan felt shame for himself and also believed that he was bringing shame on his family.

Ryan must have experienced debilitating confusion, trying to live up to the expectations his family had about the type of character he should be. This learning developed in opposition to the pressure he felt at school to fit in with other boys. When asked what he thought prompted the other boys to bully him, Ryan said: 'It was mostly because I was different'. At first, he put this down to his 'funny, sort of very religious upbringing', but he now believes that it was 'more than that. I think it was more that I was "girly" and I didn't really try to be butch'. Being 'girly' meant that you didn't like sport and were good at schoolwork. He was consequently described as a 'goody-goody' – a character not valued by other boys. By trying to live up to his family's expectations of masculinity, Ryan placed himself in the firing line of a bullying culture at school.

Failing the masculinity model: James' story

James also described emotional turmoil experienced at school – but with the added element of constant physical bullying. Aged 82, he described himself as a very shy man, although he has often been in the public eye in his work and loves to 'make people laugh'. A recurring theme in his story is the internal struggle between a private and public persona, with his 'gay self' entangled between the two. James' lived experience has been one of isolation, disappointment and rejection.

Raised in Melbourne, he now lives alone in country Victoria. He endured a very lonely childhood in a 'dreadful' suburb and recalled 'bully' teachers at his high school in the late 1940s. One teacher in particular, a former Australian Football League (AFL) 'big footballer', targeted James because he unwisely let it be known that he 'didn't like football'. James still remembers that 'when it came to hitting me one day, the teacher really landed into me with a strap. I'll never forget him'. James believes that this punishment was directly linked to his failure to demonstrate acceptable masculinity by showing an interest in, and playing, football.

Victimisation because of perceived difference and effeminacy led to trauma and confusion which still clearly impact James today. He was 'quite small' as a boy and remarked of his schooldays: 'What's the use of me? I'd get knocked over'. He now believes that this bullying by the sports teacher was partly due to his recognition that James was homosexual. Other students seemed to understand this too (even if they had little idea of its meanings); James was often called 'Sissy Brown'. He still recalls his sense of powerlessness, admitting: 'it was horrendous for me'. He 'wasn't much good' at kicking a football, and this was enough to invite suspicions about his sexuality. Although he 'loved to run and could do stuff', somehow, these other skills could not make up for his perceived lack of masculinity.

The conflation of homosexuality with paedophilia: James' story (continued) and Barry's story

James also recalled an incident from his childhood in the early 1940s that seemed to presage the difficulties he might encounter later. He remembered the punishment imposed on one of his teachers who had transgressed:

> J: My first head teacher was arrested and sent to Mont Park.
>
> D: Really? The mental institution?
>
> J: Sorry, '40, '41, '40 I was at that school.

D: Right.

J: I remember we all went up and looked at the loonies and we saw him because that was a pastime – to go and look at the loonies... it was a long walk.

D: Was he arrested for a particular incident with a child or was he arrested...?

J: Apparently, he'd been fiddling around with little boys.

What is interesting is that, when questioned about the illegality of homosexuality at the time, the story James recounted was actually about paedophilia. This is significant because it helped to shape his (mis)understanding of what homosexuality meant. He connected it to a criminal act, to mental illness and to shame. The belief in this connection was pervasive in the postwar years, with homosexuals 'frequently confused with aggressive and predatory child molesters'.[3]

Barry, 80, also described homosexuality as being somehow confused with the idea of men wanting to harm little boys

> Some stories told me or stories I read in the paper or something, that some men got into trouble with the police, but I thought it was not because of their sexuality as such – because I didn't even know what sexuality was really... but I think that I thought that it was just that they leapt out of bushes and attacked boys... or something like that. Or you would hear sometimes of a choirmaster or scoutmaster being sacked or something because of... some or something that wasn't always spelt out in my mind, but it had to do with a boy... and to a certain extent I became a bit nervous about older men, that they might want to do something to me.

When I asked whether he was perhaps connecting homosexuality and paedophilia at the time (although he didn't know the words), he paused before replying: 'Well I suppose, I suppose I must have been in some way'.

As a very young boy Barry had actually 'been approached twice by an older man, stranger'. He recalled:

> I suppose the first approach to me would have been when I was about seven, [and] the second approach not much later than that, when I was about nine maybe. Nothing happened, nothing actually... well, I don't know, one [time] certainly nothing happened, and the other, occasionally I think it nearly happened – but I was just frightened of them. They were probably nasty men.

Describing the incidents seemed to prompt new reflections. Over seven decades later, Barry realised:

> strangely I've not over the years as I think back on those, not that I think about them often, I've not really given it the name of paedophilia, but clearly that's what it was, wasn't it?

Barry was too young then to understand the difference between paedophilia and homosexuality, but this ignorance added to his sense of sex between men as being deviant and shameful, demanding suppression and concealment. It is difficult to pinpoint *how* cultural learning about connections between homosexuality and paedophilia occurred in the young boys' lives, other than through their own interpretations and experience. But such connections were erroneously made. For many years, they affected both James' and Barry's understanding of sexuality, particularly their responses to homosexuality.

Spencer, Paul, Ryan, James and Barry all struggled as schoolboys to understand the meanings of (their emerging) sexuality or homosexuality. Instead, they stumbled their way through an increasing sense of difference. Their experience taught them that being different and unable to live up to the demands of masculinity tarred them as effeminate; as less than what was expected of them. Segal says that the motivation behind this shaming by men is 'the forced repression of the "feminine" in all men'.[4] Homosexuality had no name, yet it was already influencing the boys' life experiences because of its connections with non-masculine characteristics and the devaluation of skills and interests other than sport. Perceived femininity in a man and the resulting demasculinisation process often involved mental and physical violence, perpetrated by those who held more power. At times, sexual interaction between men were also obliquely connected to paedophilia.

Realising and passing

The fear of exposure: Rory's story

Even boys who were aware of their difference and found ways to avoid censure by masking it often lived the anxious life of a 'fraud' who fears imminent exposure. Rory, 80, endured a childhood that is revealing about how history and culture exert their influence. He grew up in controlling, anti-homosexual home and school environments. When he was in Year 7 at an all-boys secondary school, Rory was aware of his difference; but, in contrast to Spencer, Paul, Ryan and James, who were unable to hide their difference, Rory became adept at deception. He realised early on that there was:

> something that I had to keep hidden – something that was shameful [because] at school there were a few people who were, I think they were probably, you know, called 'pansies' or 'sissies'.

Although Rory never thought 'I'm a homosexual', the impact of this feeling of shame was immense. He understood that he could be a 'sissy' too and that being labelled as such would make his life miserable. School was:

> very much British oriented – '*Land of hope and glory, oh valiant hearts who to your glory came*', and I suppose in a way I decided to be, you know, to conform. I just kept quiet and conformed and did what the school expected of me, and I don't know that I, whether I thought 'maybe it will go away'.

Tellingly, his housemaster's report noticed a change in his character from the time he began at his new school. Rory had transformed from 'a cheerful, cheeky person' to someone who was 'completely withdrawn'. In retrospect, Rory agrees that the description was 'very accurate'. He commented with sadness and regret:

> I think I was, would have been, you know, if somebody said, 'This person, what was he like?', they would have probably just said, 'Oh, insignificant'.

Rory is certain that the change in his personality and confidence was due to the internal turmoil he was undergoing with his sexuality. The pressure to conform was intense. He recalled one instance when heterosexual culture collided with his natural inclinations. Despite protesting against attending a school dance, he was 'sort of forced into' it. Some 65 years later, he recalled with a sense of shame and powerlessness:

> Some poor girl, the daughter of a friend of my aunty's, sort of got dragooned into going with me. I've never seen her since! The poor thing, I've often felt sorry for her.

On another occasion, Rory's friend wanted to take a particular girl to the cadet dance; because the friend had already asked another girl, he 'sort of almost blackmailed me into inviting this other girl'. Rory recalled the evening as: 'just a horror story! I hated the whole thing! I was nervous, insecure [and] probably hopeless socially'. He felt acute shame about not living up to the type of male he was supposed to be and about his lack of that sexual excitement which, he knew, other boys felt when dancing with girls.

Rory's first awakenings to his sexuality were directly connected to his failure to live up to normalised gender performance. This set up a lifelong self-doubt. He felt overwhelming shame and grief over dancing with a girl, trying to pretend that he knew what he was doing and was enjoying it. In contrast to those who could not 'pass', Rory did not present as effeminate. This probably spared him further grief. Even so, for many homosexuals like Rory, this act of 'passing' came at an enormous psychological and emotional cost. It required excruciating vigilance over language and behaviour. It created constant concern about exposure.

Questioned about the origins of his shame, Rory spoke immediately of his father and their difficult relationship. Although his father had died when Rory was 18, the older man's disapproval of homosexuals had been clear in Rory's mind when he was a young boy. He recalled that his father once referred to the popular English (homosexual) actor and playwright Noel Coward as:

> a sort of despicable person, he wasn't a real man, or something like that and the word that was mostly used would have been perv.

Without having any explicit understanding of what a homosexual was, Rory nevertheless learned that it was something to be ashamed of. It did not accord with what a man should be. He also sensed that his mother would hold similar views; she was the daughter of a clergyman and the eldest of nine children, and her attitude on all matters was 'You can't do that!! What will the neighbours think?!'

Strategising deflection: Herbert's story

Herbert, 83, was also very aware of the dangers of being labelled effeminate: 'if somebody was very effeminate, therefore they were homosexual'. Consequently, that person was bullied. The 'effeminate' boys were labelled as such because 'they were the ones that played piano...and had a cultural interest'. Herbert recalled: 'you did the opposite [of the effeminate boys], not to ever think they were going to be your friends' because to do so would risk being identified with effeminacy. He was very aware of the need to present as heteronormatively masculine. Importantly, at school and as a young adult, Herbert learned about heterosexual attitudes towards homosexuality through his heterosexual friends. Asked how this occurred, he replied:

> Well, it would come up in conversation. They would say things like, 'I think he's one of *those*', or it would be an inference that, 'Oh, he's a poof'...and at school it was exactly the same thing.

> That dreaded word, 'He's a poofter'.... you had to learn very quickly to cover your tracks. Meaning, you had to be a good actor. And you had to very carefully make sure that they were comfortable with you.

Herbert understood from an early age that any same-sex desire must be carefully hidden. Fortunately, his athletic ability in running and his 'love of sport' afforded him a means to avoid the shaming and censure that others faced. Sport was 'a great "out"': it allowed him to participate in the heterosexual world in a clandestine way, while avoiding being labelled. He was aware that he needed to be cautious, because he was also silently clear about the reasons why:

> H: In my school years, and then later on running for an athletic club, people who knew me, if they ever thought 'Oh, Herbert is very creative but he's a great sport'. And even people at school who I met many, many years later in life, 'Oh, you were a great sprinter!'
>
> D: Are you saying that being a good sprinter was a 'pass' into the heterosexual world and being accepted?
>
> H: Yes, absolutely, yes. If I said, 'I'm going to the ballet' they'd have a fit!

His recollection illustrates the power that sporting prowess afforded athletic boys. Despite his sporting skills, however, Herbert understood that he was at risk.

Herbert made the most of his knowledge of difference by protecting himself from exposure. He remained 'heterosexually male' through careful management of self-presentation, by 'choosing' interests strategically and avoiding connections with those already tainted. Even so, awareness and behavioural adjustment did not necessarily diminish emotional distress. Many homosexual boys and adults were paralysed by a constant threat of exposure, which they suffered alone. Those who were bullied, as well as those who passed, were forced to develop a remarkable resilience to survive childhood and adolescence. Some still carry the trauma.

Not realising and passing

'Where ignorance is bliss, 'tis folly to be wise' [5]: *Scott's story (continued)*

Struggle to comprehend childhood bullying, its genesis and its interpretations, formed a common thread through many of the men's stories. But the experience was not universal. A small minority managed to navigate childhood without the challenges that dormant homosexuality presented to others. Scott, 87, told one such story and was one of only six interviewees who had a relatively worry-free childhood and adolescence. Scott was unaware of his sexuality until adulthood. He did not feel any need to question his masculinity or sexuality until he was 19. Scott was adamant that he:

> wasn't even aware of homosexuality at that age. I didn't know anything about it till I was 19 [and] I was looking forward to marriage.

Now, it is difficult to imagine a world where homosexuality wasn't openly discussed. Scott's story tells us just how far from the general public's imagination it really was. Even after Scott had acknowledged his own homosexuality, he recalled:

> it wasn't until much later that I heard there was such a thing as a lesbian! It had never occurred to me that women could be homosexually inclined!

Scott's father had died when Scott was six, and his mother and three much older sisters raised him. He was untroubled as a child and was never accused of effeminacy at school. What is significant about Scott's childhood is that, despite the loss of his father at such an early age, he was surrounded by older males who encouraged him to participate extensively in different sports. Scott's youngest sister was

20 years old and married to her 25-year-old husband by the time Scott was 10. All his sisters were already married, and his brothers-in-law were all, in Scott's words, 'masculine' men who valued sporting prowess. Scott was also fortunate in that he had a very fine physique for sport. He played cricket and football and participated in athletics and swimming. During his formative years as a young boy, all three of his future brothers-in-law were frequently at the family home, courting his sisters and providing 'masculine' role models. There appears to be a direct correlation between Scott's sporting prowess and his freedom from accusations of effeminacy. Given that Scott was surrounded by women in his family, it seems possible that he may have become a target without sport and the male influence in his life. Fortunately, Scott enjoyed his school life without bullying or references to his sexuality.

Without (artificial) pointers to homosexuality, other boys and teachers apparently did not seek or detect any signs of deviancy in Scott's character. His story ran contrary to the prevalent myth that a boy or man who was homosexual was necessarily effeminate. It was possible to 'pass' at school without others doubting your masculinity or sexuality. Tellingly, Scott had the advantages of sporting ability, self-confidence and strong male role models.

Adulthood: Being who we are not, and being who we are

For a heterosexual child or adolescent, sexual awakening can be a time of frustration and uncertainty, as they seek to make sense of their emerging sexuality and learn about its cultural norms and expectations. For most, role models – mothers, fathers, brothers, sisters or the boyfriends and girlfriends of those in their friendship circle – aid the process. In the postwar era, churches and social clubs also facilitated learning about heterosexual relationships, imprinting their own conservative approach. Knowledge could be gleaned from parents, friends, ministers, popular literature and movies.

Homosexual children and adolescents had none of those advantages. In their place was ignorance, confusion, shame and an internalised message that exposure to homosexuality would be disastrous. Most homosexual adults struggled to access knowledge which only a select group of people held: those homosexuals who were confident enough to mix with other homosexuals. Knowledge was also passed on clandestinely.

Most (perhaps virtually all) homosexuals had no role models showing them what it meant to be homosexual; nor did they have relatives who were supportive of homosexuality. Written manuals and spoken advice did not exist. Private or public discussions about homosexuality rarely occurred; when they did, they were negative. Early adulthood simply continued the fear and confusion of childhood, without further knowledge or self-acceptance. Their struggle centred around being someone they were not, but they lacked insight into who they actually were.

'I'm not like other men': Colin's story

Life stories help us to account for the complexities of the circumstances that prevent the expression of who one is. Colin's story offers us some insight. He is a quiet, unassuming 80-year-old man who has spent much of his life working on a farm. He recalled that his eldest brother 'realised I was different', and consequently 'there was a lot of standing over me'. In his early teens, he understood that he was 'different', but he never really 'came out'. He had no knowledge of homosexuality and 'wouldn't have known what was coming'. Even in his mid-teenage years, when he became more aware of his homosexuality, he never told anyone: 'in a country area you would never think of it'. In later years, he did broach the subject with his mother once, telling her: 'I'm not like other men'. Her response was unequivocal: 'Oh, don't be so stupid! Don't talk like that!' The subject 'was never mentioned again'.

Community attitudes to homosexuality also affected Colin because 'what little was ever talked about was nasty, horrible stuff' spread by 'people who were important in the community'. When questioned about this type of conversation, Colin was very clear:

> D: What sort of positions did those people hold?

> C: Police and accountants, yeah. The worst ones were the cops. I just wouldn't have anything to do with them.
>
> D: Where did you hear that? In the pubs, or...? How did you hear the police saying things like that?
>
> C: Actually, in a church group.

Community and family attitudes impacted Colin's sense of self, and he fell into a deep depression during his later teens. The pervasive fear and confusion made him suicidal. Decades later, he still recalled that he 'couldn't understand it, I didn't know what to do'. In his rural community, there were no mental health services available.

Colin did not tell anyone else about his homosexuality until he started to volunteer with an AIDS organisation in his mid-40s. He recalled: 'I found I was somewhat coming home to people I could relate to'. Even so, Colin never told anyone in his circle of friends or family about his homosexuality – apart from his sister, who was 'the only one I could trust with anything'. His parents and siblings are all now deceased. Although he has many nephews and nieces, he has never been able to broach the subject with them. He was also 'really worried' because he lived near 'some ratbags..just up the road' and in 'a fairly dry area...all they need to do is drop a match on a hot, windy day and I'm gone'. Colin was convinced that his rumoured sexuality made him a target; he was told: 'you know you are being talked about a lot...and he [the person gossiping] is full of hatred'. Asked about the effect this secrecy had on him, Colin replied: 'I just lived with a cautious attitude. I didn't push the boundaries'.

Despite his later volunteer work with AIDS charities in the 1980s, Colin's life has been defined by attitudes that originated in prewar and postwar Australia. He faced persistent bullying by his older brother for being different; a stonewalling silence from his mother after his attempt to express his sexuality; threatening behaviour by his neighbours; and the knowledge that people in positions of power within his community were spreading malicious gossip about him. Remarkably, Colin remains a man of great dignity and humour. His story is one of resilience and courage. Perhaps now, in the later stages of his life, he has been able to reconcile his sexuality with his own sense of self. In response to a final question about his narrative, Colin concluded: 'I've grown a little wiser'.

Emerging from the fog: George's story
Many shared this experience of coming to terms with their homosexuality over decades. As a young man, George, now 87, trained for 18 months to become a brother in the Catholic Church. He withdrew from his studies, realising: 'this is not for me [because] the hormones were raging and all that sort of thing'. However, he did not connect this with homosexuality: 'I wouldn't have known [about homosexuality]'. Even so, he recalled that 'I sensed I was different because I could never go and join in parties with girls and that sort of thing'. George felt alienated from his heterosexual friends. He 'wasn't somehow being accepted' because 'people sensed something about me. I wasn't quite the way they were going'. In retrospect, George believes that his homosexuality was influencing his feelings and behaviour, but he had no sense of what it was or how it was impacting his experience. At the time, he felt that his friends were 'pushing [him] away by silence' and that he was 'perhaps letting myself be put in a corner'.

After leaving his religious training, George joined the army as a technical officer and remained there until he turned 40. During this time, his homosexuality began to assert itself because he was 'amongst a community of men [who were] around my age'. He realised 'in later years when I had more information that I was being discreetly propositioned by guys', but he never acted on these advances because 'I didn't know anything about it [homosexual sex] happening. I had no information whatever'.

On his mother's advice, George married at age 35, because 'sons always respect their mothers' opinions', and had children and, later, grandchildren. Although he 'would have laid my life down' for his wife, there was 'always that difference'; despite the couple having children, sex was never satisfactory. It wasn't until he was in his 50s that George began to explore his homosexuality. He joined the Victorian AIDS Council as a volunteer in the 1980s and received 'a lot of training', so 'all sorts of information came through which absolutely staggered me... and things began to fit together'. When asked what had surprised him, George's first response was that he discovered 'that men had sex with men – and it was ok! It wasn't simply a mortal sin'.

Religion, marriage and work have all played pivotal roles in George's life and shaped his life view. George's deeply held conviction that the Catholic faith was sacrosanct and that sexual acts, such as premarital sex, were sinful had made him profoundly guilty up until his late 70s. His deep faith meant:

> I [was] the worst person around...underneath I had a bad opinion of myself. I suffered the most awful guilt experiences, you know, for masturbation and all that sort of thing. If you do not confess your sin, you could go to Hell for that! I know it seems incredible – but I actually believed that!

George's understanding of homosexuality came entirely from the Catholic Church's teachings on sexuality (although homosexuality was never mentioned). In the army, he understood that it was taboo; he does not recall the word ever being used. However, he did remember that, in 1952:

> a certain couple of guys had been caught having some [homosexual] sex [and] they were discharged, virtually the next day. They were just whipped out, like that!

The only time George ever broached the subject with a priest was during this period, when he confessed that he thought he was homosexual. The priest's response was 'leave it with me'. He asked George to come back in a week, probably to allow the priest time to seek advice. The following week, George was told in confession: 'Oh! No! No! No! No! No!' George interpreted this to mean that it was not possible that he was homosexual. He let the matter drop. Yet he was aware of his homosexual desire and recalled one particular man in his army unit: 'He had a beautiful body. And I had to look away, I could see myself absolutely flaring up!' However, he was overwhelmed by shame: 'of course, guilt, guilt, came slamming in. Pow! Bang!'

Choreographing a life: Xavier's story

Xavier, 79, also illustrated some of the strategies that men used to survive as secret homosexuals. He understood that he was different to his heterosexual male friends when he was quite young. He also knew that homosexuals faced 'persecution – like being a Jew in Europe'. He recalled that '"poofter" was...the word you'd hear'. He decided early that:

> my survival technique in life was to be in total denial that anybody would think I was gay...it was a time when you really had to watch every word you said, the clothes that you wore, the way you hold your hand, everything you did was choreographed. There wasn't a minute you couldn't think. I play acted at not being gay.

Xavier's parents were 'dead working class'. Although he never told them that he was homosexual, he now believes that they probably understood. He 'looks back with eternal thanks, too late now to go and thank them, but I think how hard it must have been for them'. He took 'various guys home...and my mother, she was always really nice to them and welcoming'. But when asked if the men ever stayed the night with him, Xavier responded, 'No, certainly not!! It was inconceivable! Inconceivable!'

In 1960, when Xavier was 23, he left Melbourne – because it was 'the arse end of the world'. He chose to go to London for a couple of years because it 'had had the Wolfenden Report and it was looked on here as this paradise where you could go and breathe at last'. On his return, he was more confident in his homosexual self, and:

> life turned around and I had a lot of gay friends and after a couple of years met my partner, who I've been with for 50 years.

Acceptance and agency: Beyond the darkest decade

Many homosexuals struggled during the 1940s and 1950s. Others enjoyed life and made the most of their homosexuality. An unexpected but welcome finding of my research was that almost one-third (eight) of the 27 participants had what could be characterised as positive, fulfilled lives at some time during all or part of the postwar period. They did more than survive in a dominant heterosexual society; they thrived. Aware of the boundaries around their homosexuality, they used that knowledge to build a homosexual lifestyle that did not draw attention to itself but which, at the same time, rejected persistent expectations around marriage, children and 'settling down'.

Although the stories of the eight men were different, they often shared common features – such as a self-confidence in their homosexuality; an ability to accommodate the challenges connected with being 'the other'; a desire to seek out other homosexuals and to enjoy sociability with them; a strong sense of family acceptance – or a lack of concern about needing it; a strong sense of self as being the sum parts of more than homosexual; success in finding ways to satisfy their homosexual desire; and, finally, a sanguine outlook that prompted them to search out ways to have fun. None of these men felt the need to marry or to live up to anyone else's expectations. They enjoyed the freedoms of their sexuality. Theirs was a much broader world view that considered belief systems as part of individual choice rather than imposed state or societal constructs. This does not mean that they were 'out' in the modern sense of the word; but they did have a stronger, more developed sense of who they were as homosexuals and of how they wanted to include that understanding as they built their lives. But where did this self-belief come from, since 19 other men were unable to thrive in the same way?

No regrets: Lawrence's story
Unlike most of the other participants, Lawrence, now 75, was able to accept his sexuality early on – from age 13. Even at seven, he was 'fascinated by men' and recalled 'seeing an uncle shower. I was

fascinated by the size of his penis and pubic hair!' He became aware of sexuality in 1953 when he was 11. He was precise about the year because an older boy raped him in the library in his first year at boarding school. Lawrence was very practical and frank about the assault, explaining: 'it was a bit unsatisfying. I was a bit too young for it, I think, and I didn't sort of like the boy'. He was 'in shock for a few days'. Now, he doesn't recall it as 'traumatic' but views it as a 'turning point in life I suppose'. He recalled that he 'didn't know what was happening', but that 'shortly thereafter I certainly did!' Asked whether the experience left him wanting more homosexual sex, he responded quickly and certainly: 'Yes, of course!'

In the following years, Lawrence had homosexual sex with other boys at the school and was aware that many 'aggressively heterosexual' boys 'had boyfriends' – something that puzzled him as a child but made sense later because 'that's part of growing up I think, isn't it?' Lawrence described these relationships as 'heterosexual (male) bonding as opposed to a homosexual bonding'. He now believes that much of the behaviour was simply due to there being 'no women around' at the school. Yet, many boys did develop a homosexual bonding that remained separate from friendships:

> You're away from your home and family and you just develop attachments and over the time you become quite attached to them and become detached, then move on. There was one boy that I sort of loved and we were quite close... we were sexually experimental, but we were never close as friends.

Sex with other boys was anonymous and silent: 'we never talked to them outside of the sexual encounter'. Lawrence was adamant that the teachers were aware of the sexual activities of the boys, but they never took any action to curb the behaviour: 'the situation was not something that was discussed. It was a bit of a taboo subject'. There was a separation of sexual partner and friendship and so a disconnect between homosexuality and 'true' masculine characteristics. Unlike most of the other participants, Lawrence was unconcerned about these homosexual encounters. I asked him to speculate on what exactly allowed him to accept his sexual difference, and he was again very sure of his response.

> It didn't worry me at all because I was always self-assured, I knew who I was. I just accepted the fact that's who I was. I mean I had brown eyes, and I was the height I was, and I wasn't 6 foot 2, I wasn't 5 foot 1.

Asked whether being homosexual had made him happy, he retorted:

> That's not a very interesting question! Why would being homosexual make you happy? You're happy within yourself as a person, not because you are homosexual. It doesn't make happiness or unhappiness I don't think. I accepted that I was homosexual, and you just get on with it.

In fact, Lawrence recalled that people didn't talk about homosexuality until the late 1970s, placing the silence of the 1950s in historical perspective. During the earlier period, homosexuals had to be 'discreet' because 'there were sort of uncertain boundaries that you knew you didn't cross'. If Lawrence wanted to show sexual interest in another man, he would use his 'instinct', and 'if it was handled properly then there was no hardship'. Even when he was younger, therefore, he had an attuned sense of how to survive. Asked whether he considered himself as having a homosexual identity at this time, he said very clearly:

> I knew I had a homosexual identity... it's like having bacon and eggs for breakfast – you know, you've had your breakfast, you move on... it spanned through the course of my life.

Questioned about whether he had any regrets about his homosexual life, he was adamant: 'None whatsoever'.

A bed of bluebells: Reg's story
Perhaps past histories of homosexuality in Australia would point to

Lawrence's story as being uniquely positive; but there were others who found ways of prospering. Although Reg, 91, had lonely times when young, his homosexual life as an adult was much more positive. He 'never looked at being gay in the sense of a limitation'. Reg lives in Melbourne with his partner of 70 years. He is highly educated and was awarded his doctorate in the 1960s. He recalled:

> in the beginning of the 1940s and the war was on, I trained for some of that time as a teacher [and] I went to the teachers' college first in 1945 [and] met my partner in 1948.

He completed his 'two-year primary school teacher's certificate' and later taught in country Victoria and Melbourne, as did his partner. The pair lived together in country towns 'quite comfortably settled in' and started two drama clubs and 'put on plays'. When asked whether the townspeople knew that they were in a relationship, Reg replied: 'they could hardly fail to know', but 'never once was there a problem' with homophobia. 'In the country there was acceptance as far as we knew'. The couple also travelled extensively. Reg fondly recalled that, in the late 1940s, he and his partner 'spent a night at the New Forest, outside London, on a bed of bluebells!' On their return to Australia, Reg and his partner settled in Melbourne. Although they 'were a bit windy that they wouldn't be accepted...that was just for a period, and we got over that'. Reg was aware that homosexual sex was then illegal. He discussed it with his partner, declaring: 'I suppose you realise what we're doing is illegal?' His partner simply replied, 'Oh? So what?!' Their circle of homosexual friends grew and became a central part of their lives together.

Noteworthy about Reg's story is its ordinariness, at a time when being homosexual or living with another homosexual was far from ordinary. He and his partner lived in a domestic partnership, involved themselves in their communities, entertained, made many (largely homosexual) friends and travelled the world together. They managed to lead creative, purposeful lives by being attuned to homosexual prejudice but never allowing it to limit their possibilities.

The luxury of choice: Scott's story (continued)
Scott's homosexual life did not begin until he was around 19, in 1947. Introduced into homosexual society by an older mentor, he began to lead a life of 'music...food and dining, [and] going to eat at people's houses'. Scott, now 87, clearly remembers his pathway to his homosexual life. During his teenage years, he had no knowledge of homosexuality and 'didn't know anybody who discussed it'. But, through the 'instruction' of one man who also attended his church, St Peter's Eastern Hill in Melbourne, he became aware of his own sexuality. Scott's homosexual 'mentor' was 'careful in the way he did it' because everything was 'very secretive in those days'. Initially, Scott 'didn't mix at that time with the homosexual crowd', and 'it was *never* discussed in any form by the people that I associated with'. Slowly, he was introduced to a large circle of homosexual friends who would 'meet for social occasions and go out to dinner and all that sort of thing'. But, even then, Scott's mentor in the homosexual world 'carefully chose' the 'right' friends for him to meet – because others 'would not have suited my non-knowledge or youngness'.

Socialising with men only was a new world for Scott. He described one evening when he was dining with two other homosexual friends at an Italian restaurant next to the Comedy Theatre in Melbourne. The restaurant owners had a system for quietly introducing men to female sex workers by instructing a chosen female to sit down uninvited at the table of male customers. But the woman who sat at Scott's table soon became annoyed and pouted, complaining that he and his companions were not interested in her. One of his friends responded: 'You are quite correct! We are *not* interested in you, and we object to the management putting you at our table!' Scott laughed as he recalled how the woman then 'got up and slammed the chair into the table and walked off!'

Once Scott became part of this new, homosexual world, he found it 'fun' and avoided going to 'boring' heterosexual social events. He found the homosexual community liberating, with its absence of children and other family responsibilities. Further, he enjoyed the sexual freedom to choose when and with whom he had sex; he exclaimed:

> gay people are much more prone to living happy, joyful lives. I don't see that in straight people – they're too busy bringing up kids and trying to put food on the table. It's a different life completely. You see these women with her thumb on the blokes. The blokes want to go out and root other women... but they're not game, most of them... The gay lifestyle is much more carefree.

Scott acknowledged that heterosexual people were also having dinners and parties, but 'their parties were, you know, boring. It was the gay parties that were the fun'.

Scott was also aware of the historical positioning of homosexuality at the time. He explained:

> in those days it was, I can only speak for myself, but it wasn't necessary, I mean I was aware of my homosexuality, [but] it wasn't necessary to discuss it because everybody I knew was mixing with the other side of the fence and it just didn't come into it really.

Asked whether he preferred the secrecy of the past to the openness of the issue today, he responded:

> you can't go back, so it has to be as it is now... but it was a very straight place, way of life, that we lived, you know, from when I was born in the late 1920s. It was a terribly difficult time of course. There was, you know, all the upheaval, the industrial upheaval. People didn't have jobs and so forth and the Cold War and Korean War oh, it was just terrible. And then we got hurled into the Great, into World War II. There were lots of other sort of things too, you know. I mean homosexuality still went on, but it wasn't number one of the list. There were so many other things happening in our lives and also, at that stage, I was trying to forge a work ethic for myself and that was the most important thing, to get on you know, and buy a house and all that sort of thing.

Heterosexuals, too, were living in a world of rapid change: war, economic uncertainty and the threat of further international conflict. Homosexuality was of little immediate concern until the McCarthy era; even then, its demonisation largely played out in the USA rather than elsewhere. Scott's description points to two different worlds co-existing, yet only homosexuals held knowledge of both. Heterosexuals were largely ignorant of a lifestyle and sexuality that did not fit the postwar narrative of mum, dad and kids living in an idyllic suburban house.[6]

Of the eight participants who thrived, five (Scott, Tristan, Douglas, Francis and Lawrence) shared an indomitable self-confidence as children and teenagers. This was probably nurtured within the home; they all had happy, secure childhoods with parents who were very accepting and attuned to their needs. Two others (Reg and Henry) experienced early problems but, once they had connected with other homosexuals as adults, their lives mirrored the experience of the others. Henry was also different from the more fortunate respondents because he did not have supportive parents. Like Reg, Henry met his partner early (in 1951) and shared a lively homosexual social life with him, including 'lots of parties'. Henry recalled it as a secret world, but 'it was your community'. Harold's situation was different because he had no 'awareness whatsoever' about his homosexuality until much later in life – and yet, as a young adult, he lived a 'homosexual' lifestyle (with his wife) without the concern of facing censure himself. Instead, he shared his life with:

> all of those sort of people, who were artistic, exciting, incredible, the majority of gay men that I knew at that time were so witty, you wanted to talk to them because their repartee was amazing!

Constructing 'homosexual'

More than two decades after the period covered by this book, Altman argued that, unlike 'skin colour, or sex, or infirmity', the stigma of homosexuality is not always recognised because it can be hidden. He reasoned that 'we have to discover' our homosexuality and then 'make choices about what we do with the knowledge', because homosexual lives are 'bound up with pretence and reflection' and are about 'being who we are not'.[7] Many of the men in this book must have felt that they were accorded a role to play, that of the 'unnatural' outsider, without the characteristics of a 'normal' heterosexual boy. The perceptions of others would impact their lives negatively. Further, none of the reasons for such perceptions were ever explicitly explained. They were simply developments in knowledge that incrementally increased like pieces of a jigsaw, internalised by those it aimed to ostracise and silence.

As these men moved into adulthood, the ignorance and prejudice of others framed their development of a homosexual self. Most struggled to work out meanings of masculinity and how to live up to them. They were also wrestling with confused internal discord that lacked an affirming, comprehensible structure or signalling.

Not presenting a normative masculinity, or actually displaying effeminacy, led to accusations and disparaging terms designed to demean and shame. Constant self-management was essential. Inwardly, most homosexuals felt a troubling, nebulous sense of same-sex attraction connected to a secretive, unnamed feeling of shame.

Robert Reynolds refers to this struggle to become oneself in his discussion of gay liberation theory in the 1960s and 1970s. He quotes the work of Dr Leo Martello, an American priest and gay rights activist (1930–2000) who argued that:

> the greatest battle for a homosexual in an oppressive society was with himself... centred upon the image of himself as forced on him by non-homosexuals.[8]

This approach to a reimagining of how one could become a more self-accepting, 'authentic' homosexual is instructive, because Martello's theorising postdates by two decades the 'survival' phase of homosexual history described in this book. In 1940s and 1950s Australia, most homosexuals spent their energies avoiding exposure, arrest or committal to mental institutions. The psychological leap from survival to a questioning of heteronormative belief systems and their enabling social frameworks was gestating, perhaps, but it was still a very long way from finding a common political voice.

The preparation process for a future (unknown) homosexual life did not include positive or practical instruction from heterosexual culture, which censored nurturing and understanding of the nature of their difference and initiated a type of cultural 'non-learning'. The masculine, heterosexual world particularly dictated what was and was not acceptable by asserting its cultural superiority early in these men's lives. Learning that same-sex attraction was deviant began at home and extended into the school, workplace, friendship groups, religious, legal and medical institutions and society in general. None of this damaging instruction was explicit. Homosexuals had to find their own ways of interpreting information that initially held little meaning for them. They were challenged to create their own stories, without prompts or supportive language to guide them. Further, the people who would normally help to frame their stories – parents, friends, siblings, relatives, teachers, ministers of religion or doctors – were usually the very people who suffocated attempts at self-discovery. The impacts of unaided, negative learning frequently led to suffering in childhood and had lifelong complex consequences for many interviewees' self-identity, self-confidence and life experiences as adults.

The stories of these men are more nuanced than a simple dark homosexual history. Despite their disadvantages, men did find ways to 'become homosexual' and to acknowledge their desire and need to be with other homosexuals. They may have been denied knowledge, especially during their early years; but most still found a way to understand that they weren't alone in their same-sex attraction. At a fundamental level, this understanding came about through finding other men to have sex with – a process that is discussed in Chapter 5. Some realised that they had their parents' unconditional support, provided a 'don't ask, don't tell' approach was used. Their homosexuality could be quietly accommodated. Some men moved beyond sexual desire and found the courage to seek out social contact with other homosexuals. They were able to fashion social lives centred in homosexual 'communities' (also discussed in Chapter 5). Importantly, almost one-third of the men had a more determined, assured sense of homosexual identity, which allowed them to socialise, find sex and create a comfortable and happy life that celebrated their homosexuality.

Constructing a sense of homosexual self in 1940s and 1950s Australia was nevertheless isolating, puzzling and threatening. They lacked language to describe their attraction, faced silence about homosexuality and often felt an undefined awareness of 'difference' from normalised models of masculinity. Although most of the men knew very little about homosexuality in the period, it is not hard to find evidence of where erroneous, generalised ideas about it came from. In 1944, Harley Street London practitioner Dr Edward Griffith published a booklet called *The Road to Maturity*, in which he describes (for the benefit of other medical professionals) homosexuals as 'active' and 'passive' homosexuals, with the former being in the masculine role and 'thoroughly pernicious and in need of curing', and the latter as:

> more feminine, the result of a combination of poor hormone action in early development and a series of unsatisfactory environmental and psychological influences.[9]

Groups of homosexual men could socialise in public, but only with care and discretion

Such academic theorising about homosexuality provides a useful locale to identify contempt for effeminacy in boys and men. This fostered beliefs about sporting prowess as a proof of manhood and a lack of prowess as effeminate. Interest in other pursuits, such as reading or music, only confirmed such suspicions. Although the connection between effeminacy and homosexuality was undefined and opaque, physical and verbal bullying reinforced it. The experience of 'becoming homosexual' was further complicated and painful because being effeminate and homosexual also meant bringing shame on your family. Families often nourished this shame. Most homosexual men endured an isolated and confused childhood whose negative impacts lasted well into their adulthood. In many cases, the experience still affects their language, thinking and behaviour. (One 90 year-old potential interviewee declined because 'the government might find out').

Some fathers who returned from war were incapable of establishing

A discerning passer-by might find hints of homosexuality in body language...

a close, trusting relationship with their sons, and mothers could be just as brutal in their rejection of perceived effeminacy. The lack of a warm and close relationship with one or both parents was often exacerbated by the religious beliefs about homosexuality passed on to children. Sexuality itself had sinful connotations, so homosexuality was largely silent, undefined, yet vaguely threatening. Denial or shame were common responses. Conflict between same-sex attraction and social and religious teachings resulted in years of struggle that impacted social lives and careers.

Most men never told their parents about their homosexuality. Those who did generally faced anguish and guilt and the feeling of being a disappointment. Recognition of difference became apparent gradually to the interviewees, because they knew that they were expected to have a girlfriend and to marry, while struggling with the lack of any internal urge to do so. Ignorance and a sense of dread and personal failure magnified their feelings of confusion and loneliness.

...on the other hand, the façade might be tossed aside, even if just for a moment

As children, they tried alone to comprehend a puzzle that no one acknowledged and that had no answer. As adults, all could 'pass' in society, but 'passing' often came at enormous cost to emotional wellbeing and ability to enjoy life. Eight of the men continue to experience negative consequences from past traumas. They lack self-confidence and regret a life unfulfilled. Another 11 struggled in the early part of their lives but later built much more of a 'homosexual' lifestyle by finding community, partners and contentment.

It is even more surprising that such difficult experience was not universal. Some homosexual men responded differently to the constraints on the expression of their homosexuality. This group embraced their sexuality and the freedoms it afforded them – most especially, to ignore societal pressures to marry and have children. Homosexuality took on new meanings that paved the way for lots of fun, socialising, and the thrill of looking for as much sex as they liked. They did more than survive because they led lives that were conversely freed of normalised definitions of masculinity when in homosexual company. They enjoyed homosexual dinner parties, private house parties, socialising at 'homosexual' pubs, networking and enjoying sexual adventures with other men. None of this could be experienced in public; but this only added to the men's enjoyment. They were privy to a deliciously secret world. These men created experiences that enriched their lives.

The stories in this chapter provide evidence of pathways that emerged from an apparently interminable fog. Despite the prejudice, obstacles and dangers their sexuality presented, they were all able to 'become' homosexual – in various ways and with different impacts. They then confronted the challenge of fitting this identity into a world that saw them as criminal and aberrant. At the core of this configuring of identity was finding ways to manage self-knowledge within the confines of family, heteronormativity and marriage expectations. Chapter 4 investigates this conundrum.

4

Navigating 'homosexual': Family and marriage

The Australian postwar family

How homosexuals made sense of their sexuality and how they responded to its impacts formed one part of their experience. But other, external forces played a powerful role in shaping a homosexual's life. During the 1940s and 1950s, men were expected to marry and to start a family. Failure to do so created suspicion about loyalty to family and country, as well as doubts about a man's sexuality. So, what was the experience of the minority of homosexual men who did marry? How did most of the men avoid these expectations? How did they survive the pressures such evasion prompted?

In 1943, Anglican clergyman and Professor of Anthropology at Sydney University A. P. Elkin lamented the increasing rates of marriage breakdown during the first half of the 20th century:

> If the family is the important unit of society and a potent cultural training ground for children, the latter should be taught so from their early years, so that they will regard marriage and family as a vocation to be prepared for – not merely as something which happens.

Elkin's view that family and marriage represent a 'vocation' records the central connection of both institutions to Australian identity, a position that strengthened even more postwar. Without developed and functioning families, as well as healthy marriages that produced future law-abiding citizens, Australia would face imminent collapse. To avoid this catastrophe, Elkin advised: 'If we face the situation calmly

The ideal postwar family. Brought to you by Rinso

and practically, there need be no fear of the disintegration of the family as a social or religious unit'.[1]

World War II did not end for another two years after the publication of Elkin's book, but war had produced and entrenched radical changes in the economic, political and social make-up of the country.[2] Fears about the family led to a postwar resolve by government and its people to 'rebuild' the family after the loss of so many husbands and fathers. The 'destructive' influences of war, such as women having affairs with American soldiers while their husbands were away fighting, caused marriage breakdowns. Monogamous, committed, heterosexual love – and the nuclear family of mum, dad and children – became symbols of renewal, growth and a morally upright society. Its opposites, prostitution and homosexuality, became the 'twin evils'.[3] There was strong pressure for people to conform. Sex outside marriage was considered sinful and deviant. During the 1950s, the economic boom further nourished this ideal of the family: so marriage rates increased markedly, and young adults married earlier than they ever had before.

Mothers and fathers, secrets and silences

The (homosexual-free) nuclear family
From the late 19th and early 20th centuries, gendered roles developed as capitalist economies emerged. By the immediate postwar years, the heterosexual nuclear family was idealised as a unit of loving and sexually satisfied parents with obedient, grateful children.[4] The mother was characterised as a caring and capable housewife, the father as a responsible, hard-working husband. The romanticising of the nuclear family meant that other intimate or sexual relationships were discredited – in the case of homosexuality, even criminalised.[5]

There was no room for homosexual experience. Homosexual men generally did not aim for marriage or a sexual relationship with a woman – which automatically precluded the setting up of a household that could contribute economically to society and the procreation of children to complete the family group. They were, therefore, not only morally reprehensible and a threat; they were of no practical use to the nation. Other groups were also marginalised, including 'delinquent teenagers, unmarried mothers, divorced women, and children of divorced parents'.[6]

Tristan, 81, observed that a revelation of homosexuality 'would have brought so much shame on your family'.

Maternal and paternal warnings: Rory's story (continued) and Arthur's story

The pressure to marry and have children was often masked but also sustained. Conversely, references to the oppositional homosexual lifestyle were rare and indirect, but often brutally disparaging. Rory, 80, was never able to reveal his homosexuality to his parents. He felt deep regret for not being able to be honest with them. The topic was never broached until the 1980s. Rory recalled one conversation with his mother:

> I didn't feel that I could ever confide in her. The only time it ever came up once was she said, one night, I was in, oh, you know, I was in my 40s probably. She said, 'You're not one of *those* are you?' and to my everlasting shame I said, 'No, I'm not, and if I were, I would seek help'. I just wish I had been brave enough to say, 'Yes, I am. So what?'

When asked what his mother would have replied, Rory was sure she 'would have gone into a religious sort of fit and probably rushed around saying something about "Christ crucified!"'

Even so, while mothers sometimes reminded their sons of marriage and grandchildren, it was fathers or brothers who were more likely to deliver negative declarations about being different. Arthur's family life mirrored this pattern. Now 74, he recalled becoming aware of his same-sex attraction at 'around age 8, or 9, perhaps 12'. But this only created confusion for him during his teen years, because 'you were supposed to actually have feelings for women'. Like most men during the period, Arthur lived with his parents as a young adult. He found this 'a bit difficult' and remembered the pressure he felt from his parents to be 'normal'; 'they were always talking about [him] having a girlfriend' but he 'couldn't fulfil those ambitions that they wanted'. Whenever he went out with a female friend, his parents quizzed him. 'Oh, are you going out with "so and so" tonight? She's a very nice girl isn't she!' Arthur always felt like this was 'sort of like a "wink, wink", sort of, you know, this must be the one, you know'. He felt the unspoken inference was that his parents expected him to be heterosexual and that he should find a girlfriend, marry and have children.

Arthur's parents probably had concerns about his sexuality. Although his mother never referred to the topic, his father left Arthur in no doubt that homosexuals could not belong to a respectable family. Arthur recalled that his father once: 'had a bit of an outburst at me [and] he said he thought I was, I think it was, "a poofter."' When asked what brought on this attack, Arthur could still find some wry humour in the telling: 'I was probably having a tea party or something with my friends'. The topic was never raised again, but the lesson that homosexuals were figures of derision and disgust stayed with Arthur. Unsurprisingly, he never told his parents about his sexuality.

Arthur's story reveals the central role of language in the practice of exclusion. Apart than the school environment, the family was a principal site of derogatory language about homosexuality. This does not mean that homosexuality was a discussion topic within the family. It was taboo, only alluded to briefly through negative metaphors. Henry, 95, recalled that, because he tended to cry 'very easily', his father would reprimand him with: 'don't be such a queen':

> I didn't even, I thought, I couldn't understand why he said that, and it wasn't until I was about, maybe 15 before I happened to discover the word 'q-u-e-a-n', not 'q-u-e-e-n', and then I remember I realised that that's what he was referring to.

When asked whether he knew at the time what homosexuality meant, Henry replied, 'Not the word "homosexual". [But] I knew I was different'.

Exclusion and questions around the legitimacy of certain family members were particularly complex issues. In the first half of the 20th century, the family silenced anything that transgressed its definitions, including illegitimacy, adultery, divorce, cohabitation, criminality, domestic violence, abortion, adoption, homosexuality and lesbianism, incest, suicide, mental and physical handicaps and mental illness.[7] Notably, eight of these categories involve sexual relations, which signalled the state's and the public's interest in matters of sex, despite the silence around it. Retired High Court Judge Michael Kirby records:

> gays were not, however, the only victims of this terror [of fear and stigma] campaign: their families and friends were likewise shamed into silence. It was an age of shame and silence.[8]

There was a distinction however, between silences engineered through family 'privacy' as opposed to family 'secrecy'. A family could contain financial problems, for example, by not mentioning money concerns in public. Other issues were more complex and managed only through secrecy – because transgressions could be accessed through public documents created, for example, after births, marriages or deaths.[9] The cultural ceremonies that usually accompanied such events were also an avenue for neighbours and outsiders to glean information about other families; on such occasions, relationships between people often became evident to those seeking knowledge. Marriage ceremonies provided opportunities for others to note who did and didn't have a girlfriend or wife. Although homosexuals' families did not discuss the topic, other families sometimes gossiped about it, provided that the 'deviant' could not be connected to their own circle.[10]

Broken rites: Barry's story

In 1940s and 1950s Australia, the homosexual himself and his family ensured ongoing silence about the topic in order to avoid shame. Unlocking family secrets could have disastrous consequences. Much was at stake, including family pride; individual guilt, shame or hurt; the rewriting of history; and the reinterpreting of family stories and their meanings. Barry, 80, paid dearly for such a miscalculation. He was brought up in a very religious household. Although his father:

wasn't a nasty fellow at all...he was a man of his generation [and] he would gently...scoff at certain people whom he called 'pansies'.

When Barry was younger, he didn't know what the term referred to. He 'just thought it meant somebody who was a bit of a...sort of soft and sensitive rather than playing sport'. He recalled: 'in our family playing sport was the key to your manhood'. Unfortunately for Barry, he 'hated it from day one'. When he reached adolescence, his uncles would ask him: '"Well, Barry, have you got a girl yet?"...and all with a twinkle in their eye'. Although 'nobody was ever nasty', Barry 'could see that I was quite on another, in another world from these male cousins of mine and the other boys that I knew'.

As a young adult, Barry trained to become a Methodist minister. He recalled other homosexuals with whom he shared a certain camaraderie within the group of trainees. But that came to a frightening end when two heterosexual trainees complained that they had been propositioned: 'that started a kind of a purge as it were, well, certainly a witch-hunt'. The Warden interviewed individuals; if he extracted a confession, the trainee was immediately expelled. Surprisingly, Barry was somewhat defiant about his homosexuality and not prepared to be on trial because of it, so he made an appointment with the Warden and explained his sexuality and that he was not of the opinion that it mattered. To his relief, the Warden was 'very, very warm and understanding' and counselled Barry to return home at the end of semester to explain his sexuality to his parents, who were also friends of the Warden. Barry was assured that they would 'understand and be very supportive'. However, the response from his parents was not what he anticipated and 'caused almost a rift between me and my father', because:

> from that moment of talking to them I know that the relationship changed, and it was difficult for him [his father] to deal with me [because] he didn't know what to do with me.

His mother was 'horrified, burst into tears, and was worried about my soul'. At their insistence, he agreed to see a Christian psychiatrist to be 'cured'. He remembers almost nothing of that interview, because he was 'determined not to assist him in any way'. Unsurprisingly, Barry recalled the years from 1946 to 1959 as the 'loneliest and unhappiest period of my life'.

Although his father was a 'decent chap', Barry found his adverse reaction to his son's homosexuality devastating. He had taken his parents into his confidence but had sorely misread the depth of their negative understanding about homosexuality. He was left with a parental relationship that was badly damaged. His own religious belief system diminished, and his sense of self became vulnerable and confused. Further, he understood that his homosexuality was the cause of his parents' pain. His example records an instance where someone outside the family (the Warden) also mistakenly believed that Barry's parents would be able to set aside their prejudices and that their love for their son would help them support him.

Don't ask, don't tell: Scott's story (continued), Douglas' story, Norman's story, Lawrence's story, Tristan's story

Not all families shared the ingrained prejudices of the times. Australia in the 1940s and 1950s was still half a century away from the relative openness and acceptance homosexuals enjoy in contemporary times. However, through a family policy of 'don't ask, don't tell', some interviewees found a level of acceptance – although still with boundaries – from their families. The difference for these men was that, although they never directly spoke about their homosexuality with their parents, they had a deep conviction that their parents supported them, no matter what their sexuality. Scott, 87, had a close relationship with his mother (his father had died when he was young) and never felt rejected. Although he believes that his mother understood that he was homosexual, 'it was *never* [Scott's emphasis] discussed in any form' and 'was just something you held within yourself'. The same was true within Douglas' family life. He, too, was accepted by his parents. Yet, his homosexual life was more open than Scott's; Douglas, 76, 'never hid it. No, I didn't have to, and I didn't'. He was always aware that 'it didn't worry anybody in the family...I used to bring boyfriends [home] from time to time and they'd stay'. Douglas attributed his mother's support to her background as:

> a ballet dancer before she got married...so she must have been in contact with gay people earlier in her other life. It just wasn't an issue.

His father had his own business and had very close relationships with his male friends during the war, so he understood such bonding. He recalled his father as 'just a very nice [man] and he just accepted everybody'. When asked whether he considered such parental approval for his exclusively male circle of friends was unusual for the times, Douglas replied: 'it probably was'. It is nonetheless significant that, even in such a fortunate environment, Douglas never directly addressed the issue of his sexuality with his parents or siblings.

Norman, 88, was another participant who felt that his parents accepted his difference, although he was unsure whether they 'were thinking about homosexuals or not'. He was comfortable taking homosexual friends home to his parents, and even lived with one boyfriend in a bungalow at the back of his parents' house, but:

> it was never spoken about. As long as the person was respectable and you know, not an idiot sort of thing, they were accepting of that...You don't want to talk to, tell your parents because it's sort of not been raised ever and it could hurt them.

When asked what exactly would have hurt his parents, Norman replied: 'well, it [homosexuality] was against the law'. Even so, he believes: 'all they really wanted to know was that I was in good company and they [his friends] were responsible sort of people'. Even more unusual for the times, Norman's homosexual friends 'got on better with my parents than I did sometimes!' Norman laughed at the recollection that one day he and his boyfriend (who was living with him at his parents' house):

> had a row – only 'cause he was seeing someone else...and I said 'Well, either you go, or I go!' and he said 'Well, I don't want to go!' So, I left! And he stayed on – for quite a few years! They got on very well!

Norman initially described his parents as 'the norm' at the time, particularly because another neighbourhood family provided a similar experience:

> two doors from us there were a family, quite an ordinary family, there's three children, and I used to play tennis with them, and then we'd have a beer and Amy and Hugh would say, 'Oh, come in and we'll play cards tonight', or something like that. I'd go there every weekend, Sunday nights, Saturday and all that and there was never any thought that, or inference that that I was strange or anything. I mean they just accepted me, and we had a great time. It was sort of pretty easy really.

Asked how 'normal' his situation had been, Norman concluded his story with 'I suppose it depends on your family' – a declaration that carried profound meanings for homosexuals at the time.

Lawrence, 75, was also confident that his family accepted his sexuality, although it was 'never discussed'. He was brought up on a farm in the country and was unconcerned by his homosexuality from an early age. He thought that his parents' acceptance was not really about sexuality, but rather their willingness to embrace difference, no matter what the context. He was:

> sure that my parents, when I had grown up, were aware of the fact that most of my friends were male friends – and they were totally accepting of that.

He attributes his mother's liberal views to the fact that:

> prior to her having married my father, [she] had lived in the city

and well, she knew Ngaio Marsh for example. She knew she was a lesbian and the people she worked with, she knew there were gay people there, so it wasn't a problem.[11]

His father 'didn't sort of have any judgements on me'. Nevertheless, Lawrence never confirmed his homosexuality to his parents, because: 'whatever you did was your business'. When questioned about the common view at the time that marriage was the 'natural state', Lawrence challenged the statement:

> people either got married or they were single and there was no question about what anybody did... You know, there were a lot of spinsters around for example and a lot of things that people [said]. 'Funny he never married!' was sort of the euphemism [to suggest that a man was homosexual].

Further, Lawrence believed: 'if you were discrete about what you were doing, if it was handled properly, then there was no hardship'.

Tristan, 81, was also fortunate to have parents who supported him 'right until the day they died'. Tristan remembered declaring to his playmates at the age of six: 'I know that I will never be married'. Already, he had a very strong sense of himself as being 'different'. Even at such a young age, he was 'relating to the girls on their sort of level' and not relating to the boys. But, despite this sense of separateness, Tristan had confidence in his homosexual self by the age of 14; this, he suggests, had its origins in his parents' support of that identity:

> I was 14 when I came out to my parents, because I wanted to become a ballet dancer... I said to Mum, 'I want to go and learn to be a ballet dancer'... and she said, 'Well, you had better go and ask your father'. Anyhow, I went and said to Dad, 'Dad, I want to go and learn to be a ballet dancer' and he said, 'What for? Everybody will call you a "sissy"'... and I said 'Well, I am, so what?' and Dad said, 'Oh, ok, off you go!'

Apart from one other interviewee, Tristan was the only participant who verbally referred to his homosexuality to his parents – although, tellingly, the word 'homosexual' was not used. Asked why his father had been so accepting, Tristan explained:

> Dad had been in the war, and been a prisoner in the war, and in prisons relationships... he'd been in Changi and on the Burma railway and we know that he was very upset when his best friend died so, there was this sort of thing, that he knew that these things happened... so, he had this relationship with this man – I'm not saying it was a sexual relationship – but they had these relationships or a bonded form and he understood that this could happen amongst men. Obviously, there were people who were having sex perhaps that they knew about, you know... so he knew it could happen.

Tristan concluded: 'when I knew I had their backing I wasn't worried about what anybody else was going to say'.

A singular declaration: Francis' story (continued)
Of all 27 interviewees, Francis, 80, was the only person to directly address his sexuality with his (Catholic) parents. Although both separately and unequivocally stated their support for him, this did not mean that they discussed his homosexuality in any detail. His mother was a highly educated woman and a justice of the peace. She accepted his difference because there was 'no animosity [towards difference] because we didn't come from that type of family'.

Francis recounted the moment he told her:

> I would have been about 19 I suppose, and I said to my mother, 'Mum, I have to tell you I'm homosexual' and my mother said 'I've known that for years. Now as I was saying, before you interrupted me.'... In other words, get on with your life. Do what you're doing and don't go in for the navel gazing business.

It is remarkable (for the times) that his mother had not only understood Francis' homosexuality but had known for several years prior to his declaration. This adds weight to the possibility that mothers (and maybe fathers too) were often attuned to their sons' sexuality long before they knew themselves, but chose to remain silent on the issue. Francis was fortunate that his father also had no problem with homosexuality, saying: 'Well, your mother's told me, but we both knew anyway, so what is the problem?' Francis had served in the navy and the police force with distinction and understood that this was more important in his father's mind than his homosexuality. Further, Francis approached life with the same pragmatic attitude as his parents, remarking of his father: 'What was he going to do? What could he say? He didn't tell me I was going to burn in hellfire!' Francis recalled that both simply accepted his homosexuality and got on with life, without any need to refer to it again. He agreed that their responses were 'very unusual' for the times, 'because I know a lot of people whose family threw them out, put them on the street'. Francis attributed his mother's tolerant attitudes to her social class, education, generous nature and:

> the fact that she came from a well-connected, wealthy family. Her brother was the colonel of the regiment, and she was brought up in that era, brought up in that way – she was a professional woman herself, and she read quite a lot and got around quite a bit, and one of the judges in Queensland at the time was gay and she knew him... She was a marvellous mother!

Maternal insight and silent support: Scott's story (continued), Reg's story (continued)

Outsiders who were connected to family members in some way, such as relatives, schoolfriends, work colleagues or neighbours, were the second main source of information for families about the perils of homosexuality. Scott's first homosexual relationship began in 1959. Asked whether other people knew of the nature of that relationship, Scott confirmed that they did; he 'suppose[d] my family were aware of it – but it was never discussed'. Because homosexuality threatened the good name of a family, it could also be manipulated to exert power over not only the homosexual, but also those connected to him. Scott, 87, provided an example of such manipulation:

> I remember someone saying to my mother on one occasion, 'Now, you've got a really good-looking son but he's approaching 40 and he's never been married. Now, why is that?' And my very astute mother said 'Why don't you ask him?'

The lesson for Scott was that outsiders to the family were prepared to probe for salacious gossip through his own family members, but when the issue was as controversial as (implied) homosexuality, few would ask the targeted person directly. The story also illustrates Scott's mother awareness that she might be asked such a question and the effective rebuttal she had ready. Scott did not realise just how skilful his mother was in guarding her secret (he never openly acknowledged his homosexuality to her) until he was older. He added:

> she wasn't going to get caught up in all of that...I wasn't aware of it at the time, but I heard afterwards, many years later, that things could have been different if she hadn't been so pushy, and you know, put a stop to it sort of thing.

Although she did not say so directly, it seems likely that Scott's mother knew exactly what the outsider was intimating about her son and about her family's acceptance of his difference, and that she was prepared to defend both.

Reg, 91, told a similar story about his mother:

> My mother said when asked by some people, close friends, they said 'Oh, Mrs Lloyd, there are two things you don't know about Reg and his, his *lifestyle*' and she said 'Well, don't you worry about that – I know more than you think I know'.

In her short response, Reg's astute mother hints at her own knowledge of his homosexuality and conveys her silent acceptance of it. She also politely but cleverly slaps down the gossip her friends hope to engage in at her son's expense. Her response was also enlightening for Reg, because he could draw some comfort from knowing that his mother chose defending her son over capitulating to neighbourhood tattle that could have serious implications for her family. (Interestingly, in contemporary times, the euphemism 'lifestyle' continues to be employed, sometimes as a derogatory reference to homosexual deviancy.)

Both stories suggest that a minority of men had the tacit support of their mothers, who challenged attempts to disparage their sons' reputations. They are also examples of conversations during the era that addressed the issue of homosexuality without naming it or acknowledging its meanings. In both instances, homosexuality was an implied threat of destabilisation of the family and could be a very complex issue to manage. Scott and Reg both accepted their homosexuality but revealed it to no one within or close to their families. Their mothers (probably) understood their sons' homosexuality but chose not to divulge or discuss it – even with those sons. The outsiders, apparently, suspected homosexuality but could not name it; doing so would have crossed strict cultural conventions of inter-family and acceptable behaviour and topics of conversation. There is also the possibility that they actually knew very little of its meanings, other than as a term of shame.

Marriage: its practice and meanings

In 1940s and 1950s Australia, the family and the state exerted power through cultural definitions of marriage and the sanctioned circumstances of its occurrence. Heterosexuality was 'normal' and intricately linked with marriage as the 'sole means of sexual identity and expression'.[12] Conversely, then, homosexuality must be unnatural and a threat to the viability of race, motherhood and population. Its menace was in its power to impact the birthrate and to challenge patriarchal power. Because it did not produce children, it also threatened the very foundations of society. This made close male bonding and men who did not present as heterosexual, or who did not marry, suspect.[13] Effeminacy or remaining a bachelor past a certain age appeared dubious. In the 1950s, the pressure to marry increased, because the generation born between 1925 and 1945 (which includes all interviewees in this book, apart from one born in 1922) married at historically young ages following the end of the war – partly because of a desire to return the country to 'normal' again. Romantic love between a man and a woman was the single pathway to marriage and the only way to access sex without stigma.[14]

Marriage carried more meaning than the union of two heterosexual partners. It was 'codified as a social institution in legal, economic, social, and spiritual/religious ways'.[15] It was also seen as a safeguard of moral standards; it determined the legitimacy of, and responsibility for, children, and it protected property rights.[16] In 1949, US anthropologist George Murdock made it clear that legitimate sex meant heterosexual sex. His research did not need 'to consider so-called "unnatural practices", such as auto-eroticism and homosexuality, nor sexual sublimations such as dancing and droll stories'.[17] To Murdock, homosexuality was aberrant, strange, almost other-worldly – not worthy of academic discussion. Similarly, in his writing on marriage breakdown in Australia in 1957, the Reverend W. G. Coughlan suggests a link between sexual deviation and mental illness.[18]

In 1957, Professor Adolphus Elkin wrote in *Marriage and the Family in Australia* that:

> the goal of marriage and the family should be held...as the fundamental social vocation which none will refuse to undertake except in special circumstances.

If the present-day reader is unsure whether 'special circumstances' could possibly have included homosexuality, Elkin dispels any doubts:

> Nature and society 'call' male and female to produce and rear children who will constitute society in the next generation and cherish its culture. The affirmative response to the 'call' implies responsibility and this in turn requires training for its fulfilment.[19]

Heterosexuality and procreation for nation building and championing its culture were paramount duties of all Australia's citizens. To renounce one's duty was to repudiate one's nation and, by analogy, family, through an irresponsible ignoring of nature itself. Marriage was a hallowed institution in Australian society and carried deeply embedded cultural and symbolic meanings of duty, responsibility, mental stability and 'normalcy'. The social pressure on eligible young heterosexual men to 'marry and settle down' was constant.

So, what did marriage mean to homosexual men? Did they consider the institution relevant to them? What were its perceived benefits and drawbacks? What power did it wield over their lives, through their families, friends and work colleagues? The expectation that they would marry brought mental anguish to many, as they weighed up the consequences of deceiving everyone – not least their prospective wife.

It is easy to understand the circumstances that led seven of the men in this book to marry. The most common reasons were because 'it was expected'; due to family or peer pressure; or because 'it was [considered] natural'. Apart from George, who remained married until his wife passed away, and Harold, who is still living with his wife, none of the other men's marriages lasted. However, Terence was married for 16 years, Paul for 15, and Spencer for 11. Five of the men who married have children and grandchildren. Miles seemed to have unresolved feelings about his marriage, and Paul described his relationship with his former wife as 'a strong connection' rather than love. The other five men reported that they loved their wives, although only Bernard, Spencer and Harold connected this with falling in love. Tellingly, the same three men felt happy during their marriages. Terence engaged in homosexual sex during his marriage. He suffered psychologically as a consequence, because of his feelings of guilt. Apart from Terence all suppressed their homosexual desires during marriage.

An unconventional marriage: Harold's story
The only marriage that has endured is also perhaps the most unconventional, even by contemporary standards. Harold, 75, married

his wife when he was 23. They had five children and now have many grandchildren. He and his wife spent 'good times' together when they were younger. Both 'had so much fun' mixing with their (largely) homosexual friends in a very 'camp' world that was 'always very secret [and] very hidden'. Much of their social life was centred around parties, dinners, balls and dancing – which they found far more 'fun' than 'going to the drive-in with some boring old [heterosexual] couple'. Significantly, their lifestyle did not change even after they began having children.

Harold recalled that he 'didn't see myself as being gay, I just didn't'. Yet, both he and his wife had 'a lot of our friends [who] were gay'. These friendships played a very important part in their marriage, illustrated by a particular story Harold told:

> When my firstborn was about to enter the world... we went up to the Queen's Birthday weekend function, at Yarra Glen, you know, as many queens in Melbourne went there. There were hundreds, and they discovered suddenly that Margaret [Harold's wife] was actually in labour, so they headed this huge caravan back to the hospital where Madam gave birth. And she got cards like from, what did they call it? They used to call her 'Wally', oh I can't remember, and they called me 'Wilma' and there was a card I remember that said 'To little Wilma' and 'from aunty Pete'. It was hilarious! We had good times.

Although Harold felt that he belonged to the group of gay friends, he:

> didn't see myself as gay because the word, well the word hadn't come in, or 'homosexual', but 'camp' was what everybody called them... that was the world I lived in. That was the world Margaret [his wife] lived in. That was who we were.

Harold did not acknowledge his own homosexuality until much later in life. And although he found a much younger male lover, all three lived together in the one house for a considerable period – a testament to the strength of his marriage and his wife's resilience. During his interview, Harold's wife entered the room (unplanned) and participated in the conversation for several minutes. Both were very at ease discussing their past and Harold's homosexuality, and his wife has a friendly relationship with Harold's male lover.

Marriage as a refuge: Spencer's story (continued)

Homosexual men faced personal and moral dilemmas as they navigated family and societal expectations, Spencer, 74, had made

For many homosexual men, heterosexual marriage was a part of their history. David ('Spencer') and Heather Morgan on their wedding day November 1966

several unsuccessful attempts at having girlfriends when he was between 16 and 23 years of age:

> I sort of was always trying and it was always a disastrous failure, tiny little moments in there I'd take some girl out and we wouldn't kiss, and she'd run, jump over the fence and run back to [her] house as quickly as possible!

He wonders now whether he was subconsciously choosing girls who 'were also pretty similar about sex' – suggesting that the girls he chose were perhaps confused about their sexuality as well. Yet, Spencer did eventually marry because he 'saw that as my future'. His wife, Rosemary, was already a close friend, and they had three children in 11 years of a 'totally happy marriage'. Sex, however, seemed to be a signpost to other feelings; it was 'seriously going wrong'. Aged 36, one evening while his wife was interstate, Spencer was propositioned at a cinema by 'the most normal, nice young man', who asked whether he 'would like to go and have a drink and have some fun'. Spencer understood 'instantly what he meant and instantly knew that was all I wanted', but still declined the offer and instead 'went home and vomited, all night, didn't sleep a wink'. Not until this encounter had he ever admitted to himself that he was homosexual. The realisation altered his life from that moment. The same night, he decided that he would have to tell his wife. Even 40 years later, that memory brought emotion to his voice. He confessed to her:

> I've just had this incredible realisation that I'm gay... and I don't see how I can solve this, but I don't see that I can do anything else.

To his great surprise, not only was his wife supportive of him, but she too revealed her own homosexuality and the news that she had started to date another woman. Consequently, Spencer soon acknowledged 'this incredible urge for homosexual sex'.

Spencer still loves his ex-wife very much and has a deep friendship with her. Together, they were able to navigate issues around separation and to keep their children safe and happy in a situation that could have been very damaging to the entire family. Spencer believes that, together, they have created 'an extraordinary family and Rosemary and I get on like brother and sister now'. He has lived his life in two different worlds, as a 'married heterosexual' and as an unmarried homosexual from his mid-30s on. He is adamant, now, that he was 'never heterosexual' but rather 'a gay person just making the best I could of heterosexual sex'. In retrospect, he can 'see a very clear point between "knowing" and "not knowing" that I was gay'. He is 'happier' being homosexual because 'it's more honest'. Spencer has deeply reflected on sexuality and marriage because he saw so many others who had 'terrible problems...accepting themselves'. He is also very grateful that he has 'ended up with an extremely good family, adoring children and wonderful grandchildren'.

Perhaps a marriage such as Spencer's could be categorised as a refuge from a self-realisation of homosexuality. However, his experience suggests that the decision to marry is more complex than this. Until he turned 16, Spencer felt 'confused'. He recalled: 'I don't think I could feel anything much'. He was living in Brisbane and believes that it was a 'much more narrow-minded' city, where 'you were much less likely to come across [homosexuality] and be exposed to gay people'. By the age of 19, he had moved to Melbourne, so pressure to partner with a woman came from his peers. He also wanted to 'have sex, basically', and was 'quite frustrated' because his then religion 'sort of almost banned sex outside of marriage'. Like five of the other men in this study who married, Spencer did so at a later age than was common at the time, because he needed a lot of prompting. In later years, he felt a sense of guilt, believing in retrospect that he had probably used marriage to avoid confronting his homosexuality. He confessed:

> I feel guilty sometimes that I almost used the marriage to retain, to get through that difficult period...it was very much more difficult in those days, I suspect – much more difficult certainly than it is now in this century.

Beyond the binary: Bernard's story (continued)

Viewing homosexual history through a blunt heterosexual/homosexual binary risks missing nuances that can reveal hidden stories, as the complexity of Bernard's marriage illustrates. After the trauma of being charged with engaging in homosexual sex at age 17 and fronting court, Bernard, 74, did not touch another male 'until I was 30 or 31', despite homosexual 'fantasies – many of them'. Fortunately, he always felt at ease relating to women. Although confused as a young man, he recalled that 'women were easier' in social activities.

He 'value[s] family and children' and 'because I could engage in heterosexual activity and relate to women…I didn't feel any great deprivation'. Aged 28, he married a much younger woman because 'we were in love, and we had a good relationship'. But Bernard was aware that:

> whilst I was sleeping and fucking his sister, to be crude…I'd often fantasise about Robert, the brother and that often happened in a lot of my straight sex. I had no trouble performing with women physically, but as I was to describe to a number of people later, it's not where your cock is, it's where your head is!

Plans to start a family didn't eventuate. On an overseas trip two years later, his wife told him that she was leaving the marriage. 'My wife left me. I didn't leave her'.

Bernard then began a relationship with another woman, with whom he 'bonded both mentally and physically'. This relationship involved a lot of 'sexual activity, oh God! You know, we'd be at her house three times a week and mine four times a week!' and he 'was satisfied in that sense'. Bernard was 'not 100% satisfied – but realising probably that nobody is 100% satisfied, life's full of compromises, this wasn't a bad compromise'.

Perhaps his partner also felt less than fulfilled:

> She was a very, highly, intelligent woman and she went to Israel, she was, her family were Russian Jews in Australia. Went to Israel,

> she came back, 'cause we were looking at marriage after my divorce had gone through, and she came back and said, 'Oh, look, I've got to be honest with you – when I was in Israel I met this young lodger called Arian [and] we had this big relationship'. I was devastated, and I said, 'Well, where does it leave me?' [and] she said, 'Oh, you know, well, I'm in love with you and in love with him'. Anyway, she showed me a photo of Arian [and] he was this drop-dead gorgeous Israeli soldier, and that just fed my fantasies for months!!

A couple of months later, Bernard decided to 'call it off'. Marriage, it seemed, was not the answer. During his interview, in an ironic slip of the tongue that seemed to illustrate his conflict, Bernard concluded that he 'decided I would explore and just work out my heterosexual side – oh!! My *homosexual* side!'

Bernard now thinks that his earlier trauma at 17 contributed to his confusion and inability to acknowledge his homosexuality. 'I'd suffered so much pain by having a gay experience [that] I think in my mind the straight life was a simpler life'. He believes that he led a 'hidden life for those 15 or 14 years' of heterosexual relationships and that 'had the police not stopped [and] picked me up' when he was younger, he 'would have just evolved into a gay life'. Like many other homosexual men, Bernard struggled to reconcile his homosexual desire with the cultural and intellectual challenges of reimagining something that was so reviled.

Proof of manhood: Miles' story
In his early adult years Miles, 86:

> didn't imagine that I could be homosexual, or I should come out and be done with it or face up to it or something... although as I got to marriage by the [late for the times] age of 31 I suppose there was a doubt, certainly in my own mind. You know most young men get married around about their mid-twenties or face up to it or something even earlier, even at the age of 18.

> So [I asked myself] why didn't I get married? Why didn't I fall in love with a girl when I was 18, 21, or 24 or something?

In 1958, Miles moved into the house he still lives in. At 31, in 1962, he married 'a devout and pious Methodist minister's daughter' because 'I think I fell in love with [her] and she certainly fell in love with me'. Miles believes he too was of a similar character at the time, 'except for the sexuality area, and the politics too probably'. Eight years later, she left him, after accusing him of being 'a homosexual'. Miles recalled her parting words very clearly. She 'didn't want to hear anything or have anything whatsoever to do with me anymore because she hadn't been able to have a baby', although he had '463 times tried to make her fertile'. He recalled that 'sometimes every few months she thought...she'd conceived and she was going to have a baby'. Miles doesn't think that the lack of children was the reason behind her accusation, but rather:

> because I'd shown an interest in a book or two, a publication or two...showing I was interested in the topic [of homosexuality], along with many other topics, as you could see if you look around this room...and she walked out on me in ah, '69, about March of '69, and the issue had already become, not just political, but a bit of a social issue notably after, what's it called in New York? The...Stonewall.

Although we cannot know the reasons why Miles' wife left him, the separation points to the importance of a man's ability to father children as a demonstration of virile heterosexuality – and its opposite, an inability to father children, as an indication of homosexuality. Ironically, Miles was completely faithful to his wife for the entire period of their married life. Gittins argues that explanations of power dynamics within marriage need to be found in a 'perspective that locates them as an integral part of the socioeconomic, political and belief systems of society as a whole'.[20] Belief systems about family, marriage, fatherhood, motherhood and sexuality all collide with expectations of an idealised, happy nuclear family.

The stories above offer insights into the complexities behind homosexual men's decisions to marry in the 1940s and 1950s. They reveal the implications for both partners when the marriage failed to live up to the idealised model upheld during the era. This was, of course, also an issue that heterosexuals faced; but, although the consequences for them could also be harsh (for Catholics, remarriage in the church was impossible), the social stigma faced by exposed homosexuals was far greater. After all, divorce was frowned on; homosexuals were jailed. Harold entered what for many years was a very conventional marriage and fathered five children. His marriage has lasted and, significantly, it now accommodates his homosexuality. Spencer's marriage illustrates the dilemma many homosexual men faced between acknowledging and accepting their same-sex desire and remaining single, or masking it and succumbing to heteronormative cultural expectations. He chose the latter. Fortunately, despite the concealment by both him and his wife, they managed to have a happy marriage for 11 years. Spencer has remained very close to his former partner and his extended family.

Bernard's marriage and intended second marriage afford us some understanding of the choices homosexual men had to make. Accepting their 'deviant' sexuality and remaining single usually meant challenging parental and societal expectations and facing consequences, such as reduced promotion opportunities at work or gossip about their status or sexuality. By not marrying, homosexual men also surrendered the possibility of having children and creating their own families – something central to the aspirations of men like Bernard. Lastly, Miles' marriage suggests that, although some men married in good faith, their homosexuality nevertheless impacted the viability of their relationships. Miles intended his marriage to work, but cultural expectations about children and the creation of a happy, nuclear family, along with the hint of homosexuality, eventually affected and eroded the marriage.

Escaping marriage

'You're next!': Arthur's story (continued), Scott's story (continued), Nigel's story

What is remarkable, given the corrosive beliefs about homosexuality and the unquestioned expectation of marriage during this era, is not that seven participants did marry, but that 20 managed to avoid it. This finding appears to contradict Michael Kirby's belief that the 1950s 'were years when most gay men and women married, out of the expectations demanded of them' – although it is possible that the men who volunteered to be interviewed were more willing to confront those expectations than others.[21] Of the 20 men who never married, a few considered doing so, usually because of pressure from parents or work colleagues. Asked whether he had ever considered marriage, Arthur, 74, responded:

> Oh, yes, yes, yes! It had crossed my mind, but I thought 'How on earth could you go through the process of having children?' So, I, no, I gave up the idea fortunately.

Surprisingly, this decision did not seem to distress Arthur:

> D: Was [marriage] something that you thought about for a very long period or just a very short period?
>
> A: Oh, probably, well, probably a few years, but no, it wasn't, certainly I did it for a short period anyway, thought about it.
>
> D: Was there any pressure from either your family or outside friends, who were heterosexual, for you to marry?
>
> A: Well, mainly from my, probably my mother, 'cause if you had female friends, everybody was 'likely that somebody you would marry', but otherwise nobody seemed to worry much about it.
>
> D: But did the pressure grow as you were, for example, you know, if you think about perhaps being 22 and then you get

to 28 and you're still not married, was the pressure growing?

A: But by that stage I sort of wasn't concerned about it, I didn't worry about it then. I was a bit over it, so I just basically did my own thing without saying too much and you know, that was it.

Similarly, Scott, 87, recalled that, although he didn't feel pressure from his family, until he became aware of his homosexuality at 19, he was 'looking forward to marriage':

> it was just assumed that there would be a wonderful wedding at the church, and we all thought that way. All my boyfriends thought that we all had girlfriends and we thought that that would be eventually what would happen. So, it did happen with all of them – I was about the only one that didn't [get married].

The universal assumption of heterosexuality during the 1940s and 1950s precluded the possibility of other sexualities in the national psyche. Scott explained that 'you didn't go to somebody's afternoon tea and say, "Let's talk about gay practices"! Just didn't happen!' He added:

> people didn't know about [homosexuality] anyway. Most people, and the people I mixed with, everybody I knew thought 'Well, he's a nice catch, he'll marry some beautiful girl in the church' – and I suppose I thought that way also.

Yet, by the time Scott began acting on his homosexual desire, he 'couldn't be bothered going out with women', and marriage was no longer an option.

Navigating heteronormative cultural expectations around marriage meant that homosexual men constantly juggled the need to conceal their sexuality. At the same time, they struggled to maintain a sense of personal integrity, particularly towards unsuspecting potential wives. Nigel, 74, did not accept his homosexuality until he was 28, spending 'a good 10, 15 years alone and in denial'. He believes now that he was 'negating what really I was all about'. He remembered his mother always referring to effeminate men as 'one of *those*'. Consequently, Nigel felt pressure to 'conform', to have a girlfriend and to marry. Surprisingly, pressure came more from his work colleagues than his family, because his parents were 'good on that issue'. Although his parents 'would have liked me to [marry]', he did not experience much pressure from them. On the other hand, he recalled: 'occasionally there could be some sayings from some work people – "*You're next!*"', implying an expectation that he would soon marry. It seemed to him that 'everyone at work was getting married, and...cousins in the family were getting married'. He therefore had an 'on and off' girlfriend for about five years, 'to conform', and 'tinkered with the idea' of marriage but decided that he 'just couldn't. It would not be fair to her'. Eventually, the pressure became too much, and Nigel realised: 'I just have to get out of it'. He had 'taken her to Sydney, to Brisbane, to Hobart, to Adelaide – hotels, flights' but one day realised 'I just have to get out of it'. Consequently, on a trip to Brisbane:

> N: I asked her to have sex, and she, being a good Catholic girl, said, 'Ahhh!' [indicating shock], which I felt would be the response. Now, had she responded otherwise...
>
> D: What would you have done?
>
> N: Without question, yes, would I, or wouldn't I?
>
> D: Yeah.
>
> N: Mmm.
>
> D: So, really in your story now, there's a lost, in terms of sexuality, there's a lost decade there, isn't there?
>
> N: Yeah – and your peak years too.

Nigel's plan had worked and brought him enormous relief and increased self-confidence because he 'knew I was able to finish it'.

Eligible 'gay' bachelors: Francis' story (continued), Rory's story (continued), Neil's story

In the 1940s and 1950s, unmarried adults were still referred to as 'old maids' or 'bachelors' and regarded as somewhat aberrant. For homosexuals, the decision to marry, to consider marriage or to dismiss it was often closely connected with how they came to understand their sexuality. Sometimes this affected their personality and their ability to manage a life pathway that controverted the assumption that the only responsible choice for a single man (or woman) was to marry and start a family. Francis, 80, was the most forthright in challenging this belief system. He was able to do so because he had a very strong self-belief and also his parents' support. He understood and accepted his homosexuality very early, but he also knew that 'society, work, and their families' applied pressure on men to marry in all sorts of ways:

> trotting out sheilas for inspection, chatting away, and showing them babies and happy homes and things like that... wanting to be part of the boys. My attitude is, I don't join the boys, they can join me.

A compelling example of his approach occurred while he was working for a large corporation:

> I was working for this firm that had a head office in Adelaide [and] the Company Secretary came over and said to me, 'When are you getting married?' and I said, 'Well, I might get married tomorrow – but I might never get married. I won't get married because you're telling me. So, let's look, the Chairman's wife is an alcoholic, the Managing Director's wife is a nymphomaniac. Shall we have a look at your wife?' And that ended the conversation!

Francis was astute enough to understand the implied criticism of him as a single, unmarried (and, therefore, suspected homosexual) man who had yet to fulfil his cultural and business duty to marry. But he had also worked out how to successfully challenge his accuser and diminish the attempt to bully by linking other culturally sensitive issues such as alcoholism and nymphomania to the marriages of those in higher positions. Even so, Francis knew many men who were unable to deflect marriage expectations in the same way. He remembered:

> quite a lot, quite a lot – and the saddest part of all is those that gave in to huge pressures to get married, had children, then when they turned 40 decided they didn't want the marriage, so they ruined their lives, their wives' lives and their children's lives. There were so many of those.

Others were steadfast in their decisions not to marry. Norman, 88, recalled that, by age 17: 'I had no thought about marriage to a female and any close encounter I just reared away from it'. Lawrence, 76, simply considered it his business whether he married or not. He was unconcerned when he heard euphemisms such as 'funny, he never married', which he interpreted as 'code' for 'homosexual'. Some men thought that marrying would be unfair to the woman involved, and a few were critical of other homosexuals who chose to marry. Henry, 95, commented:

> I didn't have any of that sort of other doubts of whether I was going to come out of this [homosexuality] and I really should marry a girl, which I saw some idiots do for their own sake and for the sake of the poor woman they married. It was a totally stupid thing to do.

James, 82, was of the same opinion. He thought: 'some of these men who are gay and marry women and break the women's hearts, that's cruel'.

Not all men, however, had the confidence to decide not to marry without concern about what others would think. Tristan, 81, had more sympathy for homosexual men who married 'because of peer pressure and that's what happened a lot in those days'. He conceded, however, that 'some of those marriages turned out to be pretty bloody horrible'. He decided: 'I would never be married and most of…all my friends, were never even thinking of getting married'. Tristan recalled that 'the straight community were too busy paying off their houses, trying to get a house built and getting married', whereas for the 'gay community', it was 'party, party, party!...because they weren't interested in getting a suburban block of land and building a house on it'. Nevertheless, he found the need to strategise about how he would avoid the topic in heterosexual company:

> You learned to cope in a straight [world]...if you had a partner at the time you didn't talk about your partner. If you were in a straight society and they'd say, 'Oh, what did you do on the weekend?' And you would say, 'Oh, I just went to a party'. Cause, you didn't mention a friend or anything like that, you know. And you never mentioned, I never mentioned women's names because I wasn't going to lie. I never mentioned anything like 'dear'...

His story provides some insight into the way men were forced to be very aware of the topics they discussed and the language they used in order to avoid difficult conversations that would possibly – unwittingly – reveal their homosexuality.

Rory, 80, faced the dilemma of succumbing to family and societal expectations that a man should marry and have a family, although it went against his own sense of morality and desire not to cause harm to another person. This was a time when it was far less common for young people to move out of the family home before marriage. Therefore, by not marrying, homosexual men often had little choice but to continue living with their parents. Rory's father died when Rory was 18. His 'one older brother...couldn't wait to get away, get married and away', so Rory was left to care for his mother until he moved out at 34. He recalled that she used to say:

> Oh, you're the one who cares about me. You're the one who understands. Your older brother and your younger brother, they couldn't wait to get away.

Despite the advice of 'her sisters, a couple of them used to say to me, "For heaven's sake, get away from your mother!"', Rory was unable to do so because he 'suppose[d] I felt some obligation to her'.

Rory 'saw a psychiatrist at one stage' about feeling trapped with his mother. The psychiatrist said: 'for heaven's sake, stop going to the same church as your mother. Go to another church!' Asked whether he had discussed his homosexuality with the psychiatrist, Rory replied:

> again to my shame, he said, I think he got the wrong idea – he thought I was a candidate for the ministry and I think he was, he was sort of sussing me out, you know, and he said something about girls, and I said, 'Oh, yes, yes', and again I was too much of a coward to say, 'well, it's nothing to do with that it's because I..'.

When he was 22, Rory went out with a female colleague a few times:

> there was a girl, a woman there who was obviously very keen on me, and I liked her, she was very nice. We worked in the same office for a while, and she didn't actually say though, 'Let's get married', or 'Let's get engaged' or anything, but we went out a few times and we didn't do any, you know, no physical business. But fortunately, I knew that it was not right, it was wrong... and one of the things that I did that I'm always glad about was I said to her, 'Look, I'm very sorry but this just isn't going to work'. I never said anything about being gay. I presume she realised what it was or hoped she did because she was a nice person, I didn't want to hurt her. But I thought 'No, this is not right. I should not get married'.

Pretence or secrecy about homosexuality meant that many men were unable to openly tell their families that they would never marry. Instead, they lived for years in the knowledge that their parents hoped for an event that would never eventuate. Neil, 81, lived at home with his parents until the age of 26, when he bought a house with a [male] friend – which Neil agreed was 'unusual' in those days. Asked whether his parents were querying him about girlfriends at that stage, he replied:

> Yes, because when I took this friend home my mother made

some statement like, 'Oh, I wish you'd bring a girl home' – which really offended the other person.

Despite this awareness of girlfriends and marriage as something he knew his parents expected, Neil 'had no thoughts of getting married or having any liaison':

> By the age of around 28 it started to sink in that I would never probably be able to have a close relation, well, as I said, I took girls out for a while but there was no, didn't do anything for me, at all and I realised that then, and got a bit involved with other men.

By the time Neil was about 30, the pressure to marry began to diminish:

> I think by that time they didn't press me at all because I think they'd got used, my mother particularly, I think had got used to the fact that I wanted to have a second life but still keep in contact.

His comment hints at choices parents probably faced: causing conflict by insisting on marriage; or silently accepting the situation and still maintaining a good relationship with their sons. Neil's parents were 'pretty naïve' and referred to him as 'being one who wanted to lead a single life, or a bachelor life'. When asked whether he thought that his parents knew he was homosexual, he was 'doubt[ful]...even later in life, when I was in a relationship, they didn't query it'. Neil doesn't discount that they 'may have known – but they never, never, never said'. They did meet his boyfriends, each of whom was:

> introduced as a friend. But there was, as I said, there was no, real, what can I say? Ah, there was no, there was no intercourse [discussion] or anything like that.

In later years, Neil returned from a trip to Europe and 'did form a permanent relationship' with another man, but 'it was never discussed'.

Quizzed about what his parents knew about his partner, Neil replied: 'they didn't because we probably had our own bedrooms' so they 'probably wouldn't have thought [about it]'. Somewhat surprisingly, Neil now thinks that 'they would have been probably quite accepting [of his homosexuality]'. Even so, Neil's story was typical of the experience of many men whose relationships with their parents and extended families were compromised to different degrees. There was a perception that unmarried men did not embrace the responsibility and maturity demonstrated by marriage and children; consequently, their single (homosexual) life remained hidden and unexplained.

Hidden families

Breaking the mold: Reg's story
The meaning of 'family' is 'often based on assumptions about traditional family roles and composition, [but] increasingly has been contested in academic scholarship'.[22] Contemporary sociologists have rejected the notion of there being one universally accepted meaning of a 'family'. Instead, they refer to 'families', with newer forms created through divorce, or by gay and lesbian partners, or single parents.[23] Definitions of 'family' now account for class, race, gender and sexuality. Lesbian and gay families are 'break[ing] the mould of the benchmark family by disturbing sexist and heterosexist norms'.[24]

In postwar Australia, 'family' referred to a mother, father and children. Alternative forms were not sanctioned, including those where children of divorced parents lived in so-called 'broken families'. Unsurprisingly, the men in this book uniformly referred to their parents and siblings as their 'family' at the time. Very few lived with a male partner during the 1940s and 1950s (although many have since). Yet, the notion of a different type of family formation wasn't necessarily impossible for homosexual men who did not want to marry. For those who were comfortable with their homosexuality, life could be far from repressed.

One interviewee lived together with his partner as a family, which is proof that it was possible – but with conditions attached. The second oldest participant, Reg, 91, lived with Albert in Melbourne and in country Victoria from the late 1940s on. Reg reported: 'as far as I know there was no discussion about [our homosexuality] – we didn't hide it', but he also recalled:

> we used to have parties in East Hawthorn, and we'd put black cloths across the windows because we didn't want the neighbours to be embarrassed by a party of queens.

Neighbours looking in and discovering a large gathering of (homosexual) men in the house could possibly have led to police harassment or even arrest. Yet, again, Reg's experience did not reflect homosexual men's common fear at the time. He remembered:

> one time the police did arrive... They said there'd been complaints from the neighbours about the noise level, 'cause there was dancing, music playing. And I had my teaching job at the time in Caulfield, I was at, I had left the secondary teaching [and] I moved to tertiary teaching. That was in, I think the dates are a bit awry [so] I can't be more accurate than that. They [the police] came because of the complaints about the noise, that was all, and we were regarded as somewhat amusing.

Reg and his partner appear to have enjoyed a lot more freedom and a more comfortable life than the average homosexual man did during the times. Yet even Reg and his partner thrived by recognising that they needed to accommodate heterosexual sensitivities. Although they considered themselves as an alternative family type, it was unimaginable that the rest of (heterosexual) society would consider them as such. The need to cover their windows when hosting other homosexuals is an example of their 'family' being denied the same freedoms that heterosexual families enjoyed, such as being able to openly invite guests to their home.

Unlike Reg and his partner, most homosexual men lived with their parents until well after they reached adulthood at age 21 – as did other men until they married. Marriage signalled maturity and a readiness for independent living. Moreover, very few young people could afford their own apartments or houses. During the 1950s, as the economy grew, adult children began marrying at increasingly younger ages.

Leaving home to create a new family was clearly a heteronormatively constructed pathway that afforded no alternative models, particularly ones that involved two homosexual men living as a domestic couple. There were some examples of homosexual men living together, such as Reg and his partner, but the great majority of homosexual men did not find divergent ways of being a family. Rather, they accommodated their homosexuality within the heterosexual nuclear family – usually achieved by masking their homosexuality and concealing their homosexual social life and friends. It is sobering to note that some of the men have never revealed their homosexuality to anyone in their family.

Navigating 'homosexual'

In the postwar years, marriage and family dominated Australian life as the country rebuilt and reinvented its sense of national identity. Men were expected to work hard, provide for their wives, procreate and raise children. Compliance was a measure of masculinity. It was assumed that women would relinquish their war-time jobs for returning soldiers and that they would take on the role of domestic wife and mother.[25] Avoidance of marriage was an abrogation of responsibility.

Negative images of homosexuality usually originated within the family, particularly with fathers who conveyed their disdain of homosexual men in mocking or abusive descriptors. Shame and derogatory language ensured family silence and suffocated possibilities of alternative sexualities. Conversely, neighbourhood gossip could ruin reputations. For most, avoiding marriage was complex and stressful; constant pressure came from parents' and work colleagues' expectations. The threat of exposure and need for concealment increased as a man reached the peak marriage ages of 20s and 30s.

Often, avoidance meant carefully monitoring language and information, subjugating the self and suffering psychological distress.

For some interviewees, parental knowledge and tacit acceptance of their homosexuality made life more straightforward and uncomplicated. They enjoyed a stronger sense of self-confidence because they understood that their families did not feel shamed by their difference. They also felt more freedom, because their families did not expect them to marry. This often translated into a fun and rewarding lifestyle, without the emotional or financial responsibilities of an idealised nuclear family. Although one homosexual couple lived in an alternative family unit, it was highly unusual for the time, and they did not operate with the same freedoms or recognition as heterosexual family units. Many homosexuals certainly found ways to subvert heteronormative societal and familial expectations to search out what they truly desired – other men. However, they did so with varying degrees of success, as Chapter 5 will explore.

5

Embracing 'homosexual:' Finding the men

Conceptualising homosexual communities

Homosexual men really wanted to be with and to have social and physical sexual relations with other homosexual men; but many lived isolated lives in the 1940s and 1950s, often without knowing any other homosexuals. The search for others and the experience of sex varied markedly and depended on factors such as homosexual cultural knowledge and personal agency. In his discussion of the term 'gay' from the 1970s on, Jeffrey Weeks argues that homosexuals can find belonging in their social networks because such structures allow them to understand and survive their sexual difference through 'mutual recognition and support'.[1]

Weeks' point is pertinent to my earlier argument that we cannot fully appreciate the history of post-liberation homosexual politics, culture and social organisation without a more complete understanding of what came before. How did wider homosexual social networks begin to emerge in earlier decades? To what degree did groups of homosexuals initiate collective ways of dealing with sexual differentiation and begin to build communities based around a shared sexuality? In what settings and circumstances did mutual recognition and support first begin to develop? Were homosexual communities even accessible to all homosexuals? Is it even accurate to call them 'communities'? The answers can be found in these men's stories of their existence in a postwar social world.

Conceptualising Australian homosexual communities of the 1940s and 1950s is an imprecise proposition because of contested understanding of the term 'community'. Further, this research spans a period of change in terminology from 'homosexual' (or 'camp' or 'kamp') to 'gay' from the 1970s on. For example, 'gay community in the 1970s' can be separated from 'the old camp scene' in the preceding decades and can refer to size, visibility and political agency as features of 'community'.[2] It can also involve a group of people who have a 'sense of oneness' with each other and who 'live out the idea of community' through their relationships with each other.[3] A more contemporary definition is that it is a 'group of people who have common interests'; that it has boundaries, such as rules about membership or behaviours; that its members engage in shared activities, such as working, playing or learning; and that its members have roles and share history, experiences and time. People can also belong to more than one 'community' at a time.[4] Dennis Altman observed that 'heterosexuals often don't know a great deal about the gay world – but gay people know a lot about the heterosexual world'.[5]

A second complication is the meanings ascribed to 'community' by the participants themselves. Almost one-third (8) of the participants directly referred to concepts such as 'the straight community', the 'gay community' and 'my (homosexual) community' when discussing the 1940s and 1950s. This raises the question of perspective: how are we (or they) to know whether their use of the term is informed by a contemporary understanding or one that was different in the 1940s and 1950s? We cannot know the answer. However, the research carried out for this book did reveal that some men gathered in numbers because of their shared sexuality. I would argue that their gatherings loosely satisfy the definition of community. But it is, perhaps, enough to know that these men were meeting with each other, socialising, networking, issuing invitations to private parties, dining together, picnicking, passing on knowledge about homosexuality and having sex. It is also clear that they did not come together deliberately in order to form group identity or develop group agency. Their gatherings were not overtly political.

A final note on homosexual 'communities' concerns the restrictive frameworks around their functioning. The amount of time homosexual men spent together was constricted by their working lives, by 6 pm hotel closing times and, often, by lack of transport. Many did not own a car and could not easily travel to pubs or parties and back home again (particularly on weeknights). Public transport was less developed and less frequent than it is today. Secondly, even when they were together, their numbers only accounted for a small percentage of what we must surmise was the total number of homosexuals in Australia at the time. Thirdly, police often targeted homosexuals, which made some afraid to attend their frequently underworld and secret gatherings. Fourthly, although terms such as 'camp' were used among homosexuals, and derogatory terms such as 'poofter' or 'queen' were used by heterosexuals, descriptions of homosexuality and its meanings had no lexicon to move beyond this. Modern concepts such as 'coming out', 'gay liberation', 'gay community', 'sexual orientation', 'gay rights', 'same-sex desire' and 'gay identity' were still decades away. Homosexuals lacked the language that could help to politically frame their 'communities'.

This book accordingly identified two types of 'concepts of community': 'precarious communities' and 'social communities'. Although different, they shared common elements in that they were energised by a need for sociality, fulfilment of desire, psychological nurturing and survival. It is noteworthy that men did not necessarily remain in the one grouping. It was possible to move between the two, and many did. Factors such as age, employment situation, class, geographical location, family life, personality and chance influenced the opportunities these men had to immerse themselves – or not – in these 'communities'. The impetus for men to shift from one grouping to the other usually arose from the deepening of their knowledge of homosexuality and homosexuals. Often, this process spanned decades and extended into the formation of other communities in the decades that followed – such as gay liberation activist communities in the 1970s and AIDS carer communities in the 1980s. Prior to a discussion of the two communities, however, we need to acknowledge the particular struggle of those who could not find the connections they craved in the 1940s and 1950s.

The solitariness of the individual: James' story (continued), Henry's story, Reg's story

Simmel and (later) Bersani refer to the 'the solitariness of the individual'. It is a particularly apt description of homosexual men who had very little or no contact with other homosexuals during the 1940s and 1950s because of their own circumstances, minimal knowledge and lack of self-confidence.[6] James, 82, recounted perhaps the most poignant story to emerge from this research about the impacts of limited access to, and knowledge about, homosexual communities. He was the only participant who has never had a physical sexual episode with another man. 'Life wasn't easy at home' when James was growing up. His father was a broken man after 'the [Great] Depression and the war and everything'. He had also endured 'the shock treatment'. His mother was particularly 'straight-down-the-line'. Asked whether he could have confided in her about his sexuality, James replied sharply: 'Oh, God no!' During his teenage years, he was aware of his homosexual feelings but also knew that society viewed homosexuals as: 'a joke, silly poof, you know, 'cause it wasn't normal – which to me, it still is a bit'. Asked whether such attitudes had impacted him, James replied: 'Yes, of course'. He still struggles against presenting as a homosexual man, because:

> I know the way I sit and so forth, I do not sit like... bloody queens, [they] drive me crazy, 'cause they walk and their wrists are limp. For God's sake, stop it! And get your legs in the right position! [They] seem to be imprisoned and all of that, you know. I'm very aware of all that and I don't want to be like that anyway.

James never discussed his sexuality with anyone: 'it was mostly hidden away. It's locked inside of me, not getting near me, really, pushed it away'. At 31, he decided to move to England for four years, but his isolation and loneliness seemed to follow him. He had little contact with other homosexuals, although he did fall in love with another man. However, he described the experience as 'the most hurtful thing that's ever happened to me' because, although the other man also declared his love for James, he could not leave his then partner.

James fell in love again in his 60s. This time, the other man was already married to a woman and could not leave her. Referring to his desire for the man, James avoided using any direct description of sex and explained it simply as 'two people who really like[d] each other, but never, never did, leaving the sentence to trail off into silence. James recalled one phone conversation when his would-be lover told him: 'I've always cared for you', but 'when we were young, James, we could never be who we were'. At 68, after the man's wife had passed away, James booked 'an airline ticket to go and be with him for a week'. On the same day, however, 'the phone rang and he was killed that

Ken Lovett ('Henry'), 1950s

day [in a car accident] with his daughter and his grand-daughter'. James feels 'very bitter' about the lost possibility of a loving, sexual relationship that could have enriched his life. But, in a remark that typifies the rejection of homosexuals in another era, James summarised it as: 'mayn't have blossomed into bloody, you know, stupidity'. 'Stupidity' seems to be a forlorn summation of lost opportunity and ingrained negative learning about homosexuality. James concluded this recollection by remarking that homosexuality 'didn't destroy me entirely, did it?'

Asked whether he had knowledge of wider homosexual communities as a young adult, he replied: 'No, no, I wouldn't have known, where I lived [in the suburbs], no'. James' family life as a child and his adult years provided no opportunities for him to explore who he was or to understand that there were communities of others like him. Homosexuals like James led lives separated from homosexual communities. That prevented them from accessing knowledge about themselves and others like them.

Isolation also characterised Henry's experience in his youth and during his early adulthood, because he 'knew [he] was different'. Henry, 95, was originally from Sydney but moved to Melbourne with a homosexual friend (the only other homosexual he knew) as a young man. More than 70 years later, he found it a little perplexing to try to describe what homosexual life was like, summarising it as: 'you knew so much, yet you didn't know much at all'. Many homosexuals knew enough to understand that they were not alone in their same-sex attraction (lurid newspaper headings about homosexuality sometimes appeared) but did not know how to contact others like them. Henry could not broach the subject with family or friends, so his private homosexual persona remained a closely guarded secret to protect his reputation and safety. With no connections in the city, he and his friend felt alone: 'there was nowhere to go except where there were heterosexuals'. At this point in his life, Henry was not even looking for homosexual community because he didn't know it existed.

Often, men spent extended periods of time, sometimes years,

wondering how they could contact other homosexuals. Reg, 91, used to 'spend the whole day... pondering my position in life', while looking for men in the University of Melbourne's cafeteria. He recalls that, near the end of World War II, when he was 19, he 'fell in love with two or three different [heterosexual] guys'. Consequently, instead of dating women, as his friends were doing, he:

> used to walk around the park banging my head against a tree on a Saturday night because the person that I loved the most was going out with his girlfriend that night.

Reg found the isolation 'unbearable' and desperately asked himself: 'What's going to happen to me?' His question offers some insight into the depth of confusion which isolated men felt. They lacked the knowledge and resources that could explain who they were and how they could manage a life that did not fit the heterosexual model they existed within. Men like Reg, James and Henry often felt alone, socially isolated, sexually frustrated and confused about who they were and why they didn't meet others 'like me'.

Precarious communities: Rory's story (continued), Paul's story (continued), Henry's story (continued), Norman's story (continued), Xavier's story (continued)

Men within 'precarious' homosexual communities wholly existed in a heterosexual environment, apart from short interludes in the homosexual beat world or occasional connections with more social homosexual communities. Management of their homosexual self was much more rigid and vulnerable. Their sexuality and sexual activities provided little happiness or joy, because the individual alone largely negotiated the danger and psychological struggles they faced, without extended knowledge or group support. Men who existed within 'precarious communities' had more awareness of homosexuality and homosexual meeting places (particularly for sex) than those who were completely isolated. However, they also had limited *social* contact with other homosexuals; they did not understand how to access homosexual society or were too afraid to try. Their sense of what it meant to be homosexual was often narrowly defined around sex. This group largely included men who had sex at beats or who existed on the fringes of homosexual gatherings. Even if they were aware of gatherings, they often had scant understanding of their practices or their location. For many of these men, beat sex was directly connected to feelings of shame and fear of exposure, which meant that engaging in it brought only fleeting emotional and psychological comfort.

Heterosexuals had cultural knowledge, but homosexuals began with a blank canvas. They lacked understanding about the possibilities of homosexuality, including its communities, sex, its social practices and the locations of its culture. Seeking other homosexuals posed serious risks of arrest, loss of employment or estrangement from family. Typically, those who were able to locate homosexual communities at beats did so by chance or through the assistance of just one other homosexual man. Even when they came across knowledge, they did not necessarily know how to respond to it. Rory, 80, knew about the 'homosexual' bars upstairs in the Hotel Australia in Melbourne but didn't go to them; he 'would have been I think too scared probably'. He recalled also that he was once in the 'coffee bar in the Australia Cinema', downstairs from the Hotel Australia, and a small group of homosexual men was in there too. Rory explained that:

> I wanted, I would have liked to have been part of that...but, but, you know, the sort of inhibitions. And the, the indoctrination. was just too strong.

The memory of this occasion was obviously still painful for Rory. He recalled the scene in detail:

> R: Might have been 3 or 4 or them...they were sort of, you know, some of them were flamboyant, and um, sort of laughing and I thought, 'Oh, I wish I could join them, I wish I could join them, I wish I could be like them'. They weren't kissing or anything or holding hands. But they were obviously people

> who knew each other, and I assumed sort of met there perhaps regularly. And I just thought, 'Oh, yes, I, I wish I could be like that!' 'I wish I could join…'.
>
> D: So, you connected in, at that point, homosexuality with being open and free…?
>
> R: Yes.
>
> D: …and laughter and being yourself?
>
> R: Yes, yes! They obviously knew each other, friends, they were sort of happy to be with each other – I suppose happy being happy, laughing and joking.

Paul, 75, was raised in Adelaide and also felt very alienated from society. He was initially unable to connect with any homosexual communities because he 'didn't know there were any [homosexuals] in Adelaide'. For Paul, the 1950s was a period of complete ignorance. The process of his homosexual enculturation only began later, in the late 1960s. One man introduced him to a florist called 'Ronnie', and Paul recalled: 'through him…I was introduced to "camp" Adelaide – and I really mean "camp"!' He then met a small group of homosexuals who gathered on Saturday afternoons at the Walkerville Arms Hotel in Adelaide. Despite this introduction and his subsequent attendance at several homosexual dinner parties, Paul felt that he was included more as a tag-along guest. He 'doesn't remember going to many parties'. When he did: 'we bought the grog before' and then 'knock[ed] on the door' of a private house and 'if they recognised you, you were invited in'. The parties were 'middle-class [to] upper-class', because one man in particular was 'independently wealthy'. Although Paul enjoyed the dinners, he still felt a sense of alienation and a lack of homosexual knowledge. For example, the guests 'danced a bit', but Paul: 'wasn't aware of the other sexual stuff going on in the toilet and in other rooms – I didn't think of it'. He is 'pretty sure [he] missed cues'. Paul never really felt that he was part of a 'homosexual community'. He was 'a very private person' and found it difficult to extend his contact group.

The practice of one homosexual nurturing another's introduction to homosexual society was common – but only for those fortunate enough to connect with at least one other same-sex attracted man. While living in Sydney, Henry, 95, and his friend Sandy were also aided by an older homosexual man who provided 'a place for us to go'. Although Henry had contact with these two other men, it wasn't until he was 37 (in 1959) that he found a homosexual community; until then, he 'didn't really know' it existed. His lack of homosexual cultural knowledge is unsurprising. Henry described the postwar years as a time when 'people [were] wanting stability, wanting the mother and father and the three kids and the house'. Later, after moving to Melbourne, Henry eventually began to learn that some males lived together and that they would have 'open house at different times'. He recalled: 'in Melbourne it was a popular way of getting to know a [homosexual] community'. Becoming linked into the chain of (homosexual) information was not an organised process, but often a matter of chance meetings; but, once contacts had been made, said Henry: 'your friends that you made would tell you of other friends'.

For some men, their lack of knowledge about homosexual communities meant that sex was the only expression of their homosexuality. Participation in homosexual sex could be a dangerous activity, so tacit and secret membership of a homosexual community did not always translate into greater freedom of sexual expression or opportunity. Particularly in the working world, homosexuals had to ensure their survival by integrating, at least superficially, into heterosexual society. So the workplace became central to the practice of integration. A man's employment was an essential tool for creating a 'cover' heterosexual identity. Homosexuals who allowed their sexual desire to diminish their judgement could lose their livelihoods and reputations very quickly. Norman, 88, was very aware of this possibility. Although he was privately quite relaxed about his homosexuality, he was astute enough to understand that this sense of self did not fit the masculinity narrative his work colleagues shared. Consequently, his homosexual self was only truly expressed when he was 'in company that I felt safe'. To negotiate the different heterosexual/homosexual and workplace/non-workplace spaces, he learned to categorise those 'who were responsible, or [who were] not likely to be scandalising me [directly] or to other people'.

Although Norman had some knowledge of homosexual communities, he was especially alert to compromising situations after becoming an executive in a large firm; his more prominent profile meant much more to lose. One evening, he was walking back to the train station with a group of young trainees from his workplace after a work training session. The man who had been training the group approached Norman and boldly declared: 'I'd like to fuck you!' Sensing the danger involved in accepting the invitation, Norman instead rebuffed the younger man, replying: 'Well, you've picked the wrong time and the wrong person'. His rapid summation of the situation and his decision to choose survival over desire proved to be very wise indeed. He explained:

> two days later we were at Sandringham in a store there and a group of us...there was a young, good-looking young man, light hair, and he [the trainer] was amongst us and they...all of a sudden [the good-looking young man] was out [left the premises] and off [the trainer] went. And then, a bit later on, a phone call came for this trainer and he was out [sacked] and we never saw him again. So, he [the trainer] must have made advances to [the young man who] told his father and his father picked him up and took him in to the State Manager and the State Manager got the [the trainer] in.

Norman recalled that the trainer lost his job immediately because the father of the younger man 'didn't want him to have anything to do' with his son. Norman understood very well that the scandal was centred in 'homosexuality and the pushing of it'. While the trainer had not necessarily set out to create problems, his lack of discretion and his inability to sense how his homosexuality could be weaponised against him directly led to the loss of his job and banishment from his work colleagues – and probably trouble at home, because he 'was a married man and all that'. The incident illustrates the precarious positions in which homosexuals who operated on the edges of homosexual communities could find themselves.

Xavier, 79, was also very aware of the perils of being connected with other homosexuals and the pressure to manage knowledge. He was also in a position of responsibility in the business world and recalled the fear he constantly lived with:

> X: Every moment you were, think you were going to be...a brick's going to drop on you.
>
> D: Yeah, so it was a world of fear?
>
> X: Well, fear, yeah but it, it's very hard to convey that to people now. It was every hour of the day, every hour of the day, from the moment you got up. If somebody rang you, would they be ringing you too many times and somebody would get the impression at the office that you were getting too many calls from this man? And the worst thing, it makes your judgement of other people corrupted because you're looking at other people and these, instead of having normal relationships with other people, every, everything was sort of an air of suspicion.

Lack of knowledge was thus not the only impediment to finding and joining homosexual communities. Often, a man's position or circumstances dictated the degree of risk he was willing to take to find other homosexuals or to be seen with them. Further, as Xavier points out, trust between friends, family or work colleagues is weakened if there is always an underlying threat of an abuse of power through the exposure of compromising knowledge of another. Without secrecy, discretion and good judgement, a homosexual's search for other men could lead to ruin.

Social communities: Herbert's story (continued), Francis' story (continued), Douglas' story (continued), Donald's story, Harold's story (continued), Tristan's story

Alongside this group who lived in precarious communities, almost wholly within a heterosexual environment, was a second group, 'social communities': those with more defined, robust self-knowledge, who sought out information and locations of homosexual communities and regularly made efforts to join them. Although there was still an element of danger and daring in meeting up with other homosexuals, their desire and their self-confidence permitted them to seek out deeper meanings of what it was to live a homosexual life. Some men spent much of their private, social life purely within social homosexual communities. Consequently, they enjoyed life. Their sexuality had free expression with other homosexuals, and that made it much easier to 'play by the rules' of heterosexual society at work or in heterosexually dominated settings.

These men discovered the (few) homosexual gathering places, in bars such as the Hotel Australia. They benefited from a wider social network of homosexual contacts through (mainly) private parties and dinner parties. This group created deeper meanings of homosexuality that went beyond sex and fleeting contact. They fashioned homosexual sociability, explored its possibilities and began to build notions of collective identity and camaraderie *because of* their sexuality. In doing so, they challenged societal belief systems about their homosexuality and created 'under the radar' communities that nurtured the means for socialising and the locations in which they could thrive. In short, they were actively building homosexual knowledge, although not necessarily in any orchestrated or overtly political way. Ironically, the rules of the heterosexual world that sought to define and silence homosexuals also provided the structures around which this third group could 'be homosexual'. They provided defined parameters within which this community could nurture its members, including the spaces in which it gathered and the practices it employed (such as secrecy and codes) to ensure its survival.

Embracing 'homosexual:' Finding the men 131

Freddie Asmussen: 'probably the biggest queen that Melbourne's ever seen – but with a shitload of style and class' ('Harold')

Despite the challenges homosexuals faced in their search for other men, many did connect with social homosexual communities. Like those in precarious communities, the men who progressed to social communities made first contact through word of mouth from just one other homosexual man. In contrast, men in social communities used this initial contact to build their knowledge, to develop networks and to learn from the acquired wisdom of more experienced homosexuals. Herbert, 83, remembered that 'homosexuals couldn't be together' on the surface, but that 'these older guys...were the people that educated me in the way of life' and the threat of being 'locked up' just for being with them. He remembered that these men influenced his 'understanding of things'. One example of the survival skills they taught Herbert was the codes they employed to warn others of danger. 'Lil's out tonight', for instance, meant that 'Lilly Law' (the police) was nearby looking for 'undesirables'. Survival was closely connected with insider knowledge and helping each other. Francis, 80, (a former policeman) explained that 'we all had a patois of speech' and recalled:

> a friend of mine, he was a very handsome guy, and he had a big job. He was rattling away to somebody on the phone and when he hung up somebody rang back and said, 'Look I had a crossed line and heard what you were saying – you want to be careful what you say on the telephone'. And if the police ever got hold of you, they would take your telephone book and work their way through it, so, you never, I never write too much down at all.

> They would come around to your place and say, 'You're a poofter, come with me'. Bang! Bang!

Similarly, Henry, 95, learned that 'you didn't talk about that [homosexual community]...because you could end up being bashed'. Barry, 80, recalled: 'homosexuality itself was not thought to be "proper conversation"'; Rory, 81, agreed that it was never 'anything to really be discussed...it was still a crime...and it wouldn't have been accepted [because of] homophobic attitudes'.

Still, once connections were made, men could begin the process of learning about homosexual culture and its practices and locations. Douglas, 76, also enjoyed a fun and active homosexual life. He worked at Myer department store from around 1956, at a time when the interior design department he was part of was under the direction of well-known homosexual Freddy (sometimes Freddie) Asmussen. Asmussen was 'running the windows in those days' (interior design) and ensured that the store employed many (usually young) homosexual men. Douglas found himself in a very fortunate (and very unusually) supportive homosexual work environment that provided a ready-made community. He recalled that, as a young man, he 'couldn't get to work quick enough' because it was 'a fantastic job'. Outside work, he socialised with the same men and was able to rapidly expand his homosexual social group. Mostly, he accompanied them to the Hotel Australia 'on a Friday night for a drink'. He recalled:

> everyone was all nicely dressed up, 'cause people came from work...and you just met lots of people and you got to know different people, and different walks of life.

Once a friendship group was established, it 'just took off from there', and Douglas was invited to many after-pub parties.

In 1955, Donald, 77, was only 15. He also began working at Myer department store in Melbourne. He soon learned that it was an unusually accepting workplace because of the number of homosexual men who worked there. Later, Freddy Asmussen was the head of the 'soft furnishing department' where Donald worked. Donald recalled how fortunate he was when one of the men in the department 'took me under his wing' and educated him about homosexual gathering places and practices. He recalled that the word 'homosexual' was never used. Instead, men 'just didn't say anything' and referred simply to the 'fun, party world' – which Donald could now access because of his mentor's introductions. He learned about beats and later found others like him looking for sex in parks such as Melbourne's Como Park, in the Fitzroy Gardens and at the 'Flower Pot' underground toilet block, near St Patrick's Cathedral. (It was so called because, as Terence described, 'they had roses on top of the toilet, or geraniums' in the garden beds on ground level).

A third man, Harold, 75, also worked as an interior designer with Freddy Asmussen. He characterised Freddy as 'probably the biggest queen that Melbourne's ever seen – but with a shitload of style and class'. He was 'somebody that was really important in this kind of world that we inhabited'. Although all the participants in this book identify as homosexual, Harold's perspective is unique in that he is the only man to remain married to his wife – and still living with her (and with his much younger boyfriend). They were also the only married couple contributing to this study who moved in homosexual circles. Questioned about why he socialised in the homosexual world (while identifying as heterosexual), Harold recalled:

> there was always something a little bit weird because I was always looking at, we'd go down to Black Rock Beach and you know, most of the time... we'd sit there with a whole group of gay guys and you'd be admiring, 'Oh, he's got a really great body!'

Although Harold did not identify as homosexual in the postwar years, he and his wife were much more connected into homosexual community than most of the other participants. It was very unusual for a heterosexual couple to be members of homosexual society, so Harold's stories about homosexual community offer a singular viewpoint.

The 'homosexual' activities which Harold and his wife enjoyed mainly took place in the 1960s, but their origins dated from the 1950s. Their importance and scope increased each year. The Myer balls (which began in the 1920s) were held every year, and Harold recalled that homosexual society played a big role in their planning.[7] Those most likely to receive a sought-after invitation were famous men or those with social standing, contacts or high professional status. Harold described the ball:

> H: A huge event!... usually, put on by, I think a committee of some kind. And each year was themed and that was just all the 'A queens' were there, the whole lot. I didn't really mix in what would have been considered the 'A queen' set because they were a bit out of our league. They would have looked down on us as being a bit too arty/farty.
>
> D: Because they were lawyers or ...?
>
> H: Yeah, they were. They would have been, they were, ooo, I mean, there was one or two of them that were interior designers, even Lesley Walford in Sydney, probably the biggest 'A' queen this country's ever seen![8]

Harold also recalled frequent dinner parties:

> God knows we had at least one a week... always packed with half a dozen queens and half a dozen others – but the others would have been people who were 'sympathisers'. You brought to the table what you could – your talent, your ability, your *je ne sais quoi*, your lifestyle.

It is interesting that other heterosexuals were included in the dinner parties, because Harold was one of only two participants who mentioned this crossover between heterosexual and homosexual society. Even so, when he was asked whether he thought that many heterosexuals were aware of this alternative homosexual society, he replied:

> We tried very hard not to let them know. There were some that would know, there was no question about that, I mean there were some that just broke into that through various ways – but bearing in mind that homosexuality was extremely illegal in those days, you didn't really go out there and wave a flag.

Harold also enjoyed group picnics at the beach and recalled one visit:

> the queens organised a Sunday picnic down at Dromana I think it was and it had this slightly wrecked changing box, and it had this one pillar going up and when we arrived there, there was this dolly queen on the top of the thing, draped in cascades of chiffon floating in the breeze! It was hilarious!

Harold's extended group also had picnics in the country with 'hundreds' of 'Melbourne queens'. One particular day, they were picnicking in a field, and:

> there was a local football club, and the queens decided they'd get these footballers in on the game, so they frocked up and got on to their cars and sashayed across the thing – and all of a sudden, we were joined by 18 lusty footballers who had a ball!

Harold's stories are remarkable because they are told by someone who identified as heterosexual at the time but who was also one of few permitted into the homosexual social underworld. Many homosexuals socialised in relatively large homosexual social communities; but, as this book reveals, this world was unknown not only to most heterosexuals but also to the majority of the other participants in this book. Harold believes: 'it would come as a humungous shock to [the heterosexual world] to realise the extent and the diversity of the camp world'. This illustrates the secret nature of that world (despite its flamboyance) and the difficulties men had in accessing knowledge of its existence or of how to become a member. It is somewhat ironic, then, that Harold and his wife had (in retrospect) rather privileged membership in it.

Homosexual communities in the 1940s and 1950s offer insights into how, why, when and where homosexual men gathered and the circumstances under which they did so. Warren says: 'gay people are brought together as a stigmatised, secret group by sociability'. But, for the men contributing to this research, 'community' also carried existential meanings: connecting with others like them became part of their survival as outsiders. Questions of identity around 'Who am I?' and 'Where do I belong?' had different answers according to time and space. Being together permitted men to behave and interact in ways that released them from the pressure of constantly maintaining public heterosexual personas.[9] This included the language they used and the topics they spoke about (particularly the sexualisation of other men). When they were together, there was no need to feign sexual interest in women. Further, the relative safety and freedom of homosexual social gatherings allowed men to be less constrained about their gestures and body language. Because such communities existed under the radar, men could temporarily remove their masks and relax control of

Close male friendships forged during war or national service often lasted long after

the information offered about themselves. Bersani describes it as: 'most profoundly, the pleasure of sociability is the pleasure of existing'.[10] For homosexual men in the 1940s and 1950s, being together connected deeply to psychological and spiritual self-actualisation.

Many men were isolated because they were mostly 'outside the straight world and not within the gay one'.[11] Yet, for those who found social communities, life could be fun and exciting, although restricted by space and time. Ironically, the general populace was apparently largely content in its ignorance. Tristan, 81, recalled that, even if homosexuals were openly 'dressed up and carrying on' as 'Myer's [department store] maids', or 'playing a part of a mermaid or a fairy or something' in the Melbourne Moomba parades, 'straight people would look at that and say, "Oh, they're only actors"'. He also described how heterosexuals would 'go to the theatre for instance... and they would laugh uproariously at all the gay jokes' but 'it didn't seem to affect them because they didn't know anybody that was gay'. Tristan believes it was 'sort of an isolation for both communities [gay and straight]' and added 'the gay community were forgotten – we were not allowed to be out there'.

Invitations and initiations: hotels, bars and parties

'Homosexual' hotels and cafes

During the 1940s and 1950s, homosexuals usually gathered in numbers in only two settings – hotels or private parties. A handful of cafés played a minor role in homosexual social life, but relatively small numbers met there. In Melbourne, the most frequented bar was the Hotel Australia at 266 Collins Street, because it had several bars. Interviewees mentioned a number of other bars, including the London Hotel (Melbourne), the Sir Charles Hotham Hotel (Melbourne), Young and Jackson's Hotel (Melbourne), the Walkerville Arms Hotel (Adelaide), the Grand Central Hotel (Brisbane), Lennons Hotel (Brisbane), the Casa Manana (Brisbane), Val's Coffee Lounge (Melbourne) and the Tin-Pin Café (Melbourne).

Hotels 'were a gay beat, like a city beat... you know, the Australia Hotel for instance, downstairs was the hoi-polloi like we were, but upstairs were the solicitors and the doctors ... As Tristan reported

Spicer provides a short history of the Hotel Australia:

Completed in Collins Street in 1939 to a Leslie M. Perrott design, the Australia Hotel replaced an existing hotel of that name which had been established on the site of the highly fashionable and popular Vienna Café Hotel (1890–1915), Gunsler's Café Hotel (1879–90), and the City Club Hotel established about 1872. In 1908 the Vienna lease was acquired by Anthony Lucas, who in 1916 contracted Walter Burley Griffin to remodel the interior to form a banquet hall incorporating a balcony mezzanine for his Café Australia Hotel... The Hotel Australia became one of Melbourne's smartest society hotels and an important cultural venue and stylish meeting place. It was a favourite haunt of Americans during World War II; Sir Robert Menzies was a frequent patron and the Packer family maintained a suite there for 25 years. Both the Australia and the Royal Arcade Hotel behind it were demolished in 1989 to make way for a new hotel and the 'Australia on Collins' shopping precinct.[12]

Val Eastwood's coffee shop in Swanston Street, Melbourne in the 1950s welcomed all of Melbourne's outsiders, including homosexuals.

It is interesting to note that people in very high positions of power (including the Prime Minister) also frequented the Hotel Australia; homosexuals were gathering under the gaze of those who were members of a power structure that demonised them. Whether Prime Minister Menzies and others knew of the homosexual presence cannot be answered, but it seems probable that he would have been informed about those around him. It is also notable that US military men drank at the hotel, because homosexuals interviewed for this book reported sexual liaisons with US sailors that began there.

A sea of men. Bar culture: Douglas's story (continued), Tristan's story (continued)

Time and place played key roles in the organisation of homosexual lives and served as markers for the delineation of the public and the private. Although men who gathered together did not engage in discussions about the meanings of homosexuality (or indeed even use the word), it is clear from a historical perspective that they were, in essence, nurturing the beginnings of organised homosexual communities and identities. Drinking in a pub might seem like an ordinary occurrence today, but these gatherings represent an important symbolic period in homosexual history. Although their free time was limited after work, bar culture was important because it allowed homosexuals to discover others who shared their sexuality. It facilitated the forming of friendships and the search for sex partners.

In *Imagining the Fifties: Private sentiment and political culture in Menzies' Australia*, John Murphy reminds us that our:

> contemporary images of the 1950s exaggerate it as either dreary and intolerant, or relaxed and comfortable. But this historical perspective works through strong myths, so that 'history' becomes simply what we already 'know'.[13]

This same fixed way of viewing history is also true of our homosexual past. The popular tendency is to characterise Australia of the 1940s and 1950s as a singularly dark era for homosexuals. Yet, some men located homosexual communities and enjoyed their sexuality through social contact with other homosexual men. Even those who restricted their social life to bars often found those integral to satisfying their homosexual desire. Willett notes:

> [a] well-founded fear of victimisation certainly constrained people but, as research, memoirs and fiction from the period show, it was possible, with discretion and luck, for homosexuals to live their lives without undue harassment.[14]

Nevertheless, the experience of these men varied markedly. It depended on factors outside their meeting places, including: the degree or absence of acceptance from family; knowledge of homosexual culture, including places and practices; the influence of guilt on the psyche and, therefore, the willingness to interact with other homosexuals; their ability to employ subterfuge when needed; and the degree of fear and guilt involved either in gathering with other homosexuals or in participating in homosexual sex.

The bars attracted weekly gatherings of homosexual men. In

Melbourne, hotels such as Hotel Australia, the London, Young and Jackson's, the Windsor and the Sir Charles Hotham were frequented because they were considered stylish. The time men spent in bars was relatively short, particularly on weeknights, because drinks only began after work from five pm and concluded one hour later with the 'six o'clock swill' – the last-minute rush for drinks before the bar closed. Women were restricted in their access to bars, so male homosexuals were, ironically, provided with convenient and easy access to other men. From a heterosexual viewpoint, those in the bar must have looked like any other bar patrons in the nation – drinking, laughing and chatting together. But homosexuals knew otherwise. Not only were they creating friendship networks and sourcing invitations to private, clandestine parties; they were also 'chatting each other up' and looking for sex partners.

Douglas, 76, tapped into homosexual communities at the Hotel Australia and sometimes at Young & Jackson's or the Windsor Hotel, where he would go 'on a Friday night for a drink' with his colleagues and 'meet up with people...and plan the weekend'. He believes that the Australia Hotel became a known homosexual bar because it was 'a nice place', 'convenient' and in the 'centre of town'. The back bar at Young and Jackson's was also a place to congregate and 'look at Chloe' – a famous painting of a nude woman that still overlooks the bar area. Douglas frequented the Australia Hotel from the (under)age of 17. He remembers the bars as being very friendly and hosting a range of professions:

> you just met lots of people and you got to know different people and different walks of life. People could have been a dentist or in the clothing industry... it just took off from there.

His recollection was that some heterosexuals knew about the 'homosexual bars' and had no problem with them. This doesn't align with the stories of other interviewees, so it may be partly due to the very unusual degree of acceptance Douglas had from his parents and his work colleagues (who were also homosexual).

Tommy and sailor boyfriend

Tristan, 81, was especially knowledgeable about bar life because he worked as a bartender and was able to glean information first-hand from people he met. He frequented 'homosexual bars' often – particularly the Hotel Australia and the London Hotel. He spoke of both with fondness: 'that's where the parties started'. Contrary to Douglas' recollection, Tristan remembered with delight that 'the straight people in the lounge bar upstairs wouldn't have had a clue' about the fun that was going on downstairs and the number of men who were picking each other up for sex, because: 'you've got to remember, we were against the law'. No one used the term 'homosexual pub'; rather, it was a word-of-mouth 'message thing that sort of goes through'.

Tristan also recalled that the bars were a favourite haunt of personnel from the US Navy when their ships were in town. Often, sailors from the Australian Navy would also seek out knowledge about bars from one particular man called Frank, 'who was in the Merchant Navy [and] who was known as the "post of the coast!"' Tristan laughed as he recalled that Frank:

knew every, almost every sailor in Australia and they would just come up looking for Frank [and] because he had sailed around the coast, he knew every gay pub around the country.

Frank would direct them to the Hotel Australia, the London or the Sir Charles Hotham Hotel. Tristan added:

they [sailors] would go there and would see what was going on, and they were quite prepared for it you know. It was like an unspoken message that was where you went and then one sailor would tell another sailor if they thought it was fine for him to go there.

Tristan remembered one particular occasion when he and his friends were 'entertaining about seven of the US Navy when they lobbed in town on a ship' and explained with a wry smile that they all had a 'fun night, I can assure you!' Then:

we were invited back to lunch on board the ship the next day. There we were, there was about four of us I think, sitting with all these sailors and all the rest of it, and...the ship was open for visitors [and] they were all sitting looking at us, wondering what we had that they didn't, because we were having lunch! We didn't miss out!

Questioned about how men could be certain that they were approaching other homosexual men in the bars, Tristan remarked:

the point is that they were in a gay pub. We'd pick them up in the pub. They were a gay beat, like a city beat...you know, the Hotel Australia for instance, downstairs was the hoi-polloi like we were, but upstairs were the solicitors and the doctors and everything in the lounge bar.

If the sailors were:

short of money [in] off pay week they would, well, the Australian Navy...would come up from Flinders, Cerberus and they would go to the gay pubs and then...you would buy them drinks and they would come home.

Asked whether money was exchanged for sex, Tristan replied:

No, no, you didn't have to pay them. All they wanted was a drink and something to eat. You gave them a drink and something to eat and you could take them home.

On Sunday mornings, however, Tristan remembered:

there was another place...which was the Sir Charles Hotham Hotel...it was on the corner of Flinders and Spencer Streets... We used to have some marvellous lunches there and all, any of the merchant seamen that were in town would come in there. They would know that they could get a meal and a drink...and there'd be a floorshow, and a bloke named Siddy Brad would get up and take his false teeth out and use them as castanets and sing 'Lady of Spain, I Adore You'! And then somebody would get up and do a monologue about some funny thing that was happening, you know, and then if you met anybody that you wanted to take home you could – as simple as that!...Nothing much was said, it was all sort of done by sign language, or the gaydar would operate, you know, because gaydar is a marvellous thing!

Men would approach a sex partner for the night through 'eye contact and a smile'. Tristan's approach was to say: 'Come on home and we'll open a couple more drinks'. It was 'very free and easy', although most men were respectful in doing this. Such invitations were aided by 6 o'clock closing, which continued throughout the 1940s and 1950s (licensing laws remained unchanged in Victoria until 1966).[15] Melbourne did have some nightclubs, such as New Claridges and Ciro's, but none was permitted to serve alcohol. They were structured around dancing and dining – which assumed the clientele to be heterosexual.[16] There was nowhere else to go other than private parties – unless you were fortunate enough to have an apartment, which few did.

Perhaps surprisingly, despite the shared sense of struggle among homosexuals, the bars they frequented still mirrored existing class divisions. Douglas, 76, recalled that one of the upstairs bars at the Hotel Australia catered mainly for professional homosexual men who dressed in 'jackets and suits, collar and tie' and who met on Friday nights after work. The downstairs bar was mainly reserved for homosexual 'rough trade', masculine working class men who sometimes had sex with professional men. Other than for sex, there was little mingling between the two groups. Harold, 75, also remembered 'a queen set of "in-crowd"' homosexuals in both Melbourne and Sydney. Francis, 80, reported that, when he was in Brisbane in the 1950s, the main homosexual gathering place was the Grand Central Hotel; it was for 'the better class of person', such as 'the ballet people and the opera people and...a whole lot of premier dancers...[who] were straight'. This was also the only instance when an interviewee commented on a mixing of homosexual and heterosexual men in the same bar.

Behind closed curtains – party society: Herbert's story (continued), Xavier's story (continued), Henry's story (continued), Tristan's story (continued)

Hotel bars certainly provided spaces for socialising, networking and finding men to have sex with after closing time. But a further important function of the bars usually occurred just before they closed: the issuing of invitations to private house parties afterwards. These parties offered opportunities to meet and further cement friendships with other homosexuals; provided a space for sexual liaisons and a safe environment in which to negotiate them for another time and place; facilitated a deeper sharing of homosexual cultural knowledge; and, importantly, allowed homosexuals to relax and have fun.

Private gatherings of homosexuals ran the risk of police raids. Invitations were usually through word of mouth, and addresses remained otherwise secret. But Herbert, 83, revealed another method for issuing invitations. As a young adult, he was introduced to 'homosexual' bars through a work colleague:

> I went up to what was then called the Travel Bar, and here is a whole group of young guys all dressed in their business suits, and you could tell as they drank a little bit, and the tongues were being loosened up a little bit that you were with a whole crowd of fun loving guys and... it wasn't till I got home that night, and I was taking things out of my pockets and I had a little invitation. If I wasn't doing anything, would I like to come to a party that Saturday? And it was signed [by] a particular person that I had met at that pub!

The invitation had been extended without Herbert noticing at the time. On the night of his first homosexual party, he recalled arriving at a house to find all the windows and doors shut – but music playing inside. Herbert stood for a while thinking, 'Gosh, I hope I've got the right place, I'll look an awful fool if I've got the wrong place!' But then:

> I pushed the buzzer and the music stopped from inside the house, a door opened, and I said, 'I've been invited by such and such to come here', the door was opened, music went back on, and everybody flooded around me to say 'Hello!', and I suddenly realised I was at a gay party!

Herbert also recalled that men making arrangements on the phone about attending a party would use female pseudonyms to avoid suspicion. Gay men socialising with each other often used female names too, but not everyone agreed with this practice. Xavier, 79, for example, found it 'demeaning and stupid'. He perceived an element of 'self-loathing' and 'a confusion' in its use, because 'nobody knew what to do – they had no role models whatsoever'. However, Herbert explained further:

> H: It was a period also that if you were meeting somebody away

Private homosexual parties were havens for relaxing and letting one's hair down

from those parties, they may ring you, and quite often if that same person was on the phone, you might use a pseudonym, a female's name.

D: Mmm, are you saying that when you were on the phone, and you were talking to another gay man and trying to perhaps set up a meeting...

H: Yep.

D: Were you using a pseudonym so that, for example, your parents or someone else who may have been listening wouldn't...?

H: I didn't do that myself.

D: Right.

H: But that the older friends of mine did.

D: They did.

H: Of that period. I was, perhaps a little braver than that.

D: Yes, that you learned from older gay men, that you had to be very careful?

H: Absolutely!

This was the beginning of an enjoyable, fun and exciting time in Herbert's life, as he discovered the homosexual world of the postwar era. Herbert also discovered that he wanted sex. At parties he 'met people and at that period, then went to their places'; he couldn't take men back to his home, because he lived with his mother. Sex was:

> therefore, centred on rendezvous at [other men's] places at their flats... in the South Yarra area, [where] most gay guys you met came from.

Herbert found the men-only parties exciting: 'everybody danced for fun [and] drinks of course and lavish foods!' Having been a dancer, Herbert 'always knew the latest steps of everything, and particularly Latin American at the time [so he] very much met so many people'. The parties became a liberating revelation for Herbert during:

> a time of finding that alcohol and sex was not very good for me because I found that I wanted sex, thank you very much!

Men in this study reported that the parties ranged from small groups to around 15 people and were usually only attended by homosexual men. Although there was a strong homosexual presence at events such as the Myer ball, it was ostensibly a heterosexual event. Smaller house parties revolved around food, cigarettes, drinking, dancing and sex. Party hosts were always alert to the noise level; if police were called and found a house full of men, everyone could face harassment or arrest.

Contrary to the commonly held perception of Melbourne in the 1940s and particularly the 1950s as a conservative, heterocentric and dull city, Henry, 95, recalled that 'there were [homosexual] parties in Melbourne practically every weekend if you were in the know!' Tristan, 81, described the importance of such parties in his own experience:

> D: So, when you look back, in this research period, would you say that you lived mainly in a homosexual world, apart from the fact that some of your workmates would have obviously been...?
>
> T: Well, you worked in a straight world. You were in the, I am more in the gay world now than what I was then.
>
> D: Are you? Right.
>
> T: Yes, yes, because in that, in that period, in that era, everybody was, as I say, was this work ethic thing, you got, you kept, went and got work, and you worked, where you were working was basically straight, you know, so you, you learned to cope in a straight thing. The only thing is that if you had a partner at the time you didn't talk about your partner. You know what, if you were in a straight society and they'd say 'Oh, what did you do on the weekend?' and you would say 'Oh, I just went to a party'. 'Oh, good, ok'. 'Cause, you didn't mention a friend or anything like that you know. And you never mentioned, I never mentioned women's names because I wasn't going to lie. I never mentioned

anything like 'dear' or whatever you know – that wouldn't have entered my mind. I just said 'No, I just went to a party'.

D: But it does sound like you spent, even though you say you're perhaps involved with the gay community more now...

T: Mmm.

D: but it does *sound* like you were...

T: Oh, we were!

D: having a good time!

T: Oh, we were still pretty big in the gay [homosexual] world in Melbourne back in those days because we, it was just one of those things, well, we met this Frank, as I say the 'Post of the Coast' and he introduced us to so many people and what have you, and we had, we just had a ball!

D: Would it be correct then, or not correct, to say that looking back at that time, that in some senses the gay world is not very different? It was certainly there and very strong at that time. Just, the only difference nowadays is that it's far more open and...

T: That's, that's... It's probably correct, it's probably correct. But we used to have dinner parties and house parties and I can remember having a house party where there were 100 people there and Channel 9 arrived! With the news!

D: Why did they arrive?

T: Because we had people from a stage show, I think, I can't remember what was on, it was at Her Majesty's [Theatre] and I knew some of the people in the cast. And we had a party for them. And it was a huge party! And it was a lot of fun!

Parties in private homes provided 'a very camp' world that was 'always very secret [and] very hidden' (Harold)

> D: So again, what really intrigues me, but in a nice way, is that people tend to think, and this is where I perhaps started with my whole research, people tend to think that the 1940s and '50s was very repressive for homosexuals, but it doesn't sound like your experience was repressive.
>
> T: It wasn't! No. Look, you can't keep human nature down. And being gay is a human nature and you can't keep it down. You'll always find your society. You will always find your group.

These parties provided an outlet from the strict self-censorship that homosexual men maintained during the week within their families and at work. But, like the gatherings in bars, they also carried a deeper cultural significance, even if this was not particularly evident at the time. Homosexuals receiving invitations and being able to attend parties and meet lots of homosexual men learned that they were not alone; their sexuality was much more common than generally believed, and many men accepted their homosexuality and used the ignorance of the rest of society to their advantage to lead secret but fun-filled lives.

For many men, the concept of homosexual survival therefore took on a broader meaning. Henry realised that he became much happier in himself after he began attending parties. Although they were secret, men could 'come out' to each other within the confines of the party house and revel in the freedom of expressing who they were without immediate danger. For those lucky enough to find a way into this underground world, the impact of the parties on their wellbeing was enormous. Henry recalled:

> when you realise that you're not the only one, there are hundreds of you, that's when you begin to discover that there's a completely different community.

Party communities had beneficial psychological impacts. They cushioned some of the subterfuge men had to employ in other (heterosexual) social situations. Most men lived with their parents in their early adult years, so they had to be adept at covering their tracks even in their domestic life. Each time Xavier got home after a party, his parents would greet him with, 'Oh, you've been to a party! Meet any girls there?' Xavier would reply 'Yes, lots!'

Celibacy, beats and meanings of sex

In his discussion of sexuality during the 1950s in Australia, Murphy says: 'the postwar period is easily mistaken for one of sexual denial'. However, he disputes a reading of the era as one in which sexuality was silenced. Instead, he argues that 'commentators' discussed sexual adjustment widely. As we have seen, sexuality was only ever discussed within the parameters of marriage – and was, therefore, singularly heterosexual in its meaning.[17] The implications for homosexual men's understanding and experience of sexuality was profound. Of these 27 men, only seven mentioned heterosexual sex. Significantly, those seven were the only participants who married prior to acknowledging and acting on their homosexual desire. None of the other participants engaged in heterosexual sex or had any desire to do so.

For most homosexual men, the desire for homosexual sex was even stronger than laws, inhibitions and fears. Most did find sex, although the circumstances and the reward varied immensely. Apart from their psychological barrier, men had to resolve two problems: how to find a willing partner and where to have sex. In 1940s and 1950s Australia, most adult children did not move out of the family home until they married. Although the 1950s saw the movement of some young people away from their parents to live in apartments, few of the interviewed men lived away from home during their early adult years. Most did not have access to a private space. Homosexual liaisons were usually arranged, or took place, in four main settings: bars, private house parties, cinemas or beats. Sex could be arranged in bars but did not occur in them, because they were not exclusively homosexual, and fear generally prevented restrooms being used.

In terms of sexual expression, the men in this study can be divided into four different groups. The first group included those who had very little or no homosexual sex at all in the 1940s and 1950s (although all bar one did so in later decades). The second group found sex at beats, such as public toilets and parks, but also suffered psychologically from the guilt and fear connected to such sex. The third group largely confined their sexual expression to beats but differed in that, although 'doing the beats' was still a furtive and dangerous activity, they actually found the illicit and secret nature of beat sex to be exciting and the risk alluring. The final group included men who were relatively comfortable with their homosexuality and who embraced their desire for sex with other men. This created more opportunities for sexual liaisons. Unsurprisingly, the group each of these men belonged to was closely connected to the community they accessed.

Involuntary celibacy: James' story (continued), Rory's story (continued), Ryan's story (continued)

'Involuntary celibacy' refers to men who, during the 1940s and 1950s, were unable to act on their homosexual desire because of heteronormative cultural learning and lack of opportunity. These men remained celibate during the period; marriage and heterosexual sex were not options they ever considered. James, 82, was the clearest example of the corrosive impacts of negative homophobic conditioning. He was the only interviewee who had never enjoyed the sensation of his body against another man's body in a sexual act. Although he was aware of his homosexual feelings as a teenager, he nevertheless 'had girlfriends' – but there was never any sex: 'everything wasn't promiscuous in those days, so you didn't get up to much'. He was a 'disappointment' to his father because of his poor sporting ability. He also recalled that homophobic bullying made his school years 'horrendous'. His early understanding of homosexual sexuality arrived when he was about 15 and had started to work. Each day, there was 'a man in the train who used to be very free with his hand'. But the experience was far from comfortable, because the man 'was a bit of a creep'.

James described himself as 'very, very shy'. This prevented him from doing anything more than 'looking' at 'someone attractive'. Asked about sex, James quietly replied that there was 'none, just none'. He recalled only one possible opportunity to engage in sex when he:

> was in Queensland [and] someone invited me back to their room. Nothing happened. His landlady was in and yelled at the door: 'Have you got someone in there?!' Not that I was going to anyway.

The possibility of sex grew more and more problematic. In his later years, James was overtaken by a sense of futility around longing for sex: 'I wasn't playing. Life's been a bit of a shit in many ways'. The missed opportunities for sex and relationships weigh heavily on James in his 80s. He concluded the discussion of sex with: 'I do regret the fact that in my whole life I never had anybody'.

In young adulthood, Rory, 80, also lacked confidence and struggled with his homosexuality. He realised when he was at high school that he 'was different', and he became 'completely introverted'. The only time an opportunity for sex presented was when he was around 18 and:

> went down to St Kilda one night on my own and I was sort of approached in a public toilet and oh! I was horrified! So, I turned around and came home again. Scared I think, scared. I don't think I was excited. I think I was just, 'Oh, this isn't sort of something I want to be involved in'. I don't know whether I was, probably scared more than horrified, yeah.

In his late teens, he used to go to a 'coffee bar' at the Hotel Australia, because 'there were people there…that I categorised them, I knew they were gay'. But although Rory 'knew that there was something going on that I wanted to be a part of', that 'this was me in a way', he was never 'brave enough to sort of go up and talk'. Rory must have felt insecure and fearful as he approached the café and then sat watching other men, unable to approach them and paralysed by the shame connected to his homosexuality. The impacts on Rory's sexual experience have been profound. It wasn't until 'the first time [he] went overseas…and watched a video in a sex shop in Munich', when he was 38 (in 1976), that he even understood how men could have sex with each other. Rory recalled: 'I could not believe that men did those things with each other [and] not only that, but they actually were filmed doing it!!' After this revelation, he continued his travels in London and described his experience as: 'Wow! Did I have a time!' Despite his new-found sexual knowledge, Rory did not tell anyone that he was homosexual until 1993. Sexually and emotionally, Rory feels that 'there's this sort of feeling of all those wasted years, but anyway, that's you know, you can't wind things back'.

Suppression of homosexual desire during the 1940s and 1950s was a common narrative. Ryan, 76, was 'probably between 13 and 14' when he understood that he was attracted to other boys. He 'had a hard time at school' because of his difference but 'kind of just denied it' because it 'would have been unacceptable to even think of myself as being gay'. His confusion at the time is evident in his description:

> I mean I think that in one way I was quite convinced that I was, that I was different, and that I was homosexual, that I um, I found boys particularly attractive, that I, they were what I fantasised about, they were what I masturbated about. You know even masturbation was another issue for a Baptist.

When asked whether he would have acted on his desire in early adulthood if the opportunity had presented, Ryan responded: 'probably not. I would have been too inhibited'. He 'didn't actually act on [homosexual desire] until I was 27 years old'. His repressed sexuality, his lack of sexual confidence and his scant knowledge of homosexual cultural practices kept him celibate for almost 15 years:

> D: If you take those periods you were talking about, the early years of high school...what opportunities for sex did you take up during those periods?
>
> R: The only opportunities for sex I had during those periods were my right hand. Mmm.
>
> D: And that was right up until your later medical years, was it?
>
> R: Yes, it was. I really, you know, it sounds incredible, but I had absolutely no, no physical contact with a guy...throughout my high school years, my...
>
> D: And early uni?
>
> R: Early university and late university.
>
> D: Right. Had the opportunity presented itself in the later high school years, do you think you would have taken it?
>
> R: Probably not, I probably would have been too inhibited... to do so. I was, the first opportunity that came my way, was

late at night, on duty at my hospital at Concord. Concord Hospital was an old army hospital and there was a big, modern new block. Do you know Sydney at all?

D: I know Sydney a bit, but I'm not that familiar with the hospital.

R: Right, then down beyond the hospital were the old, all these old ramp wards. They were called ramp wards, they were, which had been established during the Second World War because it was a big military hospital then. They were all connected, they were just sort of prefabricated type buildings, which were connected by ramps and most of the land was reclaimed, mangrove swamp – in fact right down the end there were mangrove swamps, into the Parramatta River, and sometimes late at night you'd get called to one of these outlying wards…and there was a nurse, male nurse who was exceptionally sexy! And who, and they all used to

Melbourne's public toilets were intended as conveniences; they were certainly a convenient place for men to meet

wear nice white uniforms in those days, and often when I'd get called, to you know, when you're on call to go down to one of these wards, which was usually to certify some poor old guy who'd died...walking back this guy would, would come out of whatever ward he'd been looking after, and he'd been smoking a cigarette (laughs) and looking kind of alluring! And I always thought 'God, he's sexy!', you know... and passed him, and it was only later that when I was talking to Frank, the guy who'd been a psychiatrist at Concord, and talking to him about it, he said, 'Oh, that guy, he used to boast about the number of doctors he'd got off with' you know, at night! But, I mean, perhaps he didn't find me terribly attractive, 'cause he never put the hard word on me! But if he had of, I'd probably would have!

Apprehensive beat sex: Barry's story (continued), Terence's story, Colin's story (continued), Francis' story (continued), Herbert's story (continued)

Weeks argues that the meanings we give to sexuality are socially organised. Although he doesn't dismiss the role of biology, in that it determines what we can or can't do, he concludes that sexuality itself is 'a product of negotiation, struggle and human agency'.[18] Men searching for sex who did not access homosexual communities in bars or at parties frequented the only other option available to find sex: beats. Homosexual beat sex usually took place in public toilets, parks, isolated car parking areas or bushland along secluded riverbanks or beaches. It is a clear example of negotiation, struggle and human agency colliding, as men mediate the type of sex on offer; its location; its timing and duration; the inclusion of verbal exchanges or not; how it is initiated and how ended; how many participants engage in it at the same time; who takes an active or passive role; the degree of aggression involved; the psychological excitement or fear it generates; and the need to be alert to the danger of being bashed or charged with criminal offences.

For most men, the search for sex was far from psychologically or practically straightforward. Even among male homosexuals, beat sex is often characterised as an almost desperate, last resort; Dalton notes that it: 'attracts much legal, social and cultural hostility as "dirty" sex that is out of place, repulsive, disgusting and offensive'.[19] But a lack of knowledge about homosexual communities, gathering places and 'pick up' practices drives the fear, uncertainty, shame and guilt that often intersect with the search for sex. Many (although not all) of the men who chose to 'do the beats' had no other options for finding sex. They did not gather in 'homosexual' bars or attend private parties. Beats had to be places where men frequently visited (such as public toilets) or 'beat' cinemas (mainly in the immediate postwar years) or concealed public areas. Some men also had sex in cars, but few owned a vehicle in the 1940s and 1950s. Although the sex that took place in beats provided a physical and emotional release, it also carried the threat of being bashed or arrested by the police. Worse, it carried the danger of exposure through gossip, innuendo or the media.

Some men found beat sex too confronting, too dangerous or simply not the way they wanted to have sex. Paul, 75, always found that beat sex left him 'frustrated', because 'there is no deeper connection' with the other partner. Others, like retired minister Barry, 80, had a great deal of sympathy for those who used beats. Such visits were not only connected to sexual longing; they also spoke to the loneliness men felt when they desperately wanted to make connections with homosexual communities they couldn't find:

> I was very cross with a lot of gay people who scorned those who did the beat. I'm a great defender of people who do the beat regularly, having been myself. Lonely people do and when there's not ways in society for more easily making contact with people and having opportunities for sexual occasions, and that really was just about the only opportunity.

The search for sex is interwoven with our desire for human connection.[20] It involves being physically intimate with another person and enjoying the pleasures of another's body. Weeks also says that it is about 'what goes on in the mind and in society' and is 'shaped and embedded in social life'.[21] Participants in this book illustrated these connections. Terence, 86, spoke of the link between the longing for emotional contact with other men and having sex with them in beats. In 1956, at 25:

> I had nobody to talk to...inside you got that feeling that you have to be with somebody. I don't think it was so much I have to be with sex, you know...just to cuddle somebody...and that's all.

Terence was brought up in Europe and migrated to Australia as an adult. He married a woman 12 years older, a choice he explained by musing: 'I suppose I was looking for a mother figure because my mother died when I was 12 years old'. Until he separated at around 45, it was 'not a happy period'. He was 'struggling with the right thing to do', trying to negate his homosexual desires. He did not find social homosexual communities and suffered for the lack of them. Anonymous beat sex was challenging, because it did not help him to understand the meaning of his same-sex desire. Consequently, he felt alone and at a loss in his search for knowledge. He also felt guilty about deceiving his wife. Although he 'had homosexual feelings since I was 12', he was still:

> very frustrated that when you're looking for something later on you know where to look and what, and you're still...very lonely. You were cut off somehow...I remember I went to Innsbruck...I went through the streets for four hours crying because I was alone. I didn't know was it I was crying because I was homosexual, or was I crying because I was alone? I had nobody to talk to. I was about 25.

Terence was very candid about his knowledge and frequenting of Melbourne's postwar beats. He attributes his need to use them to three different reasons: 'the urge' to have homosexual sex; a need to prove 'that I'm a man' by taking the top (active) role; and the lack of alternative ways to find sex with other men – 'there was nothing else you know'. Terence 'went to the beats all over the place' and was familiar with at least 10 in the inner city of Melbourne, including:

> three in Flinders Street, one in top of Russell Street, one right by the Flinders Street Station going down, and then one under the viaduct, up, Flagstaff Gardens, Faraday Street, and then the one in the 'Flower Pot' (public toilet).

With sexual release, he also experienced guilt, because he was married and because he was engaging in homosexual sex. Sometimes he convinced himself: 'no, don't do that [go to beats] and then for a few months there was nothing'. His same-sex desire perplexed him. He could not understand: 'why does that thought [desire] always come back to you?'

Colin, 80, also suppressed his desire for homosexual sex. He was in his 'mid-teens', around 1952, when he understood that he was homosexual. Not until the 1980s (when he was around 45) did he speak to anyone else for the first time about his sexuality. During the 1950s, Colin 'wasn't active' in seeking out sex:

> I just didn't want to – I don't think I felt the confidence to do anything…I played around a bit I suppose but nothing more than that.

Asked why he hadn't attempted to have physically intimate sex, Colin replied that he was 'wary' at first; later, 'it became real fear'. Consequently, his mental health declined.

In later decades, Colin 'had occasionally gone to the beats' in the Melbourne suburbs of Melton and at Footscray Park, because the men he met there were:

> good, sensible, usually married men – but they were very fair, sensible and intelligent people and you could talk and not be in any way put down…I got real support out of that.

Unfortunately, Colin discovered that the affirming nature of beats could also change. They could very quickly become very dangerous, and one occasion (in the 1980s) had life-changing impacts on him, Colin approached a man in a public toilet and would have liked him to 'give me a hug, a bit of comfort'. Within seconds, Colin found himself being severely bashed by the two policemen who had entrapped him. They subsequently charged him, yelling 'fucking filth' at him. Although the incident took place three decades after the postwar period of this research, it highlights the profound and deeply ingrained homophobic attitudes that prevented men from freely expressing their sexual desire in the postwar years and beyond.

Violence perpetrated against homosexuals at beats could make sex life threatening. Xavier, 79, described police bashings as a 'blood-sport'. Francis, 80, (the former policeman), recalled that, in order to avoid being caught, 'you just had to watch yourself' – which he was very capable of doing:

> I was up drinking at the British Empire [Hotel in Brisbane] with a friend of mine, this guy was chatting us up and he said 'Would you buy me a bottle of Scotch?' and I said, 'Sure', and I bought the Scotch and he said 'Now I'm going to take it off you, you poofter bastard', and I said 'You really want it don't you?' He said 'Yes', so I said 'Here it is! Whack!' and then myself and my friend fled down the back stairs!

Even so, he remembers:

> There were a lot of terrible bashings. A very good friend of mine was attacked in the park and he had a metal band on and they pulled it off and took all the skin off there, and another guy was picked up by a gang and they put a milk bottle up his rectum, and when I picked up the paper you'd look at it and 'this one was killed and that one was killed' and you knew what was going on. A lot of gay bashings.

Even if perpetrators were apprehended, the outcome for the

homosexual victim was never positive:

> D: Did those, to your knowledge, did the people who were bashed, did they go to hospitals for treatment?
>
> F: Oh, yes! They had to! I went in to see one they did that to, and I didn't even recognise him he was so badly attacked.
>
> D: And was anyone ever charged in those cases?
>
> F: They were. They charged the lot that had the milk bottle – but of course then the guy [the homosexual victim] had to leave the state because everyone knew who he was.

Alluring beat sex: Francis' story (continued), Henry's story (continued), Herbert's story (continued)

Many doing the beats experienced dangers and a lack of emotional connection, but others found the challenge and the rewards of anonymous, freely available sex to be an adventurous and self-empowering pleasure. Francis, 80, educated himself about beat culture and places by talking to other homosexuals. Taking account of this firsthand knowledge, he was cautious when using beats, but the chase and his own agency in finding sexual partners also excited him. He sometimes chose to 'cross' between social homosexual communities and the anonymous beat environment. He was also one of the few men in this study who was confident and unconcerned by his sexuality. Although he was still careful about his behaviour and his immediate environment when searching for beat sex, he felt no guilt – which was even more notable because he had always had a very strong religious faith. Francis knew what he wanted and went out to find it! In his former work in the police force, he had to be particularly careful when looking for homosexual sex, but this did not stop him at all. He was astute enough to carefully separate his public and private lives. Francis also knew that he had some protection from his police colleagues:

if you're living with other men and playing sport with them and playing cards with them and showering with them, horsing around with them, you don't approach them sexually. Basically [they] won't believe that you're homosexual because they all think that they're God's answer to everybody else! It's as simple as that!

During his early adulthood Francis worked in Brisbane and knew of 'the famous beat called "The Fig Tree" – where you went if you wanted to meet blokes'. Asked how he knew about the beat, Francis recalled that his heterosexual police work colleagues unwittingly educated him about the places 'where the poofters go'. Francis explained: 'you stood on the street until you saw somebody going into the lavatories that you fancied, and you went in after them'. The first time he went,

Loitering with homosexual intent or just hanging around? Sex could often be found in public places

when he was 18, was the result of a conscious decision he had made to 'go and get a bloke'. After making his choice at the public toilet, Francis and the man drove to the river because it was surrounded by bushland. Most men 'did it in the bush' or on the banks – partly because it was safer, but also because 'most people had no money, so it would never occur to [us] to book into a hotel or to rent a flat'. Francis remembered that his mother asked him the next morning:

> 'What were you doing last night?' I said 'I don't know Mum' and she said 'Well, there's cow manure all over the back of your best suit!' I had been rolling around on the banks of the river with a law student – who went on to become an Ambassador for Australia!

Asked how he felt about the experience, Francis replied ironically: 'I probably thought I could improve a bit!'

For Henry, 95, the gaining of knowledge was slower and less transparent. Nevertheless, he had no qualms about using beats. He was quite practical in his approach to searching for sex and 'though it was secret, there were certain ways that you could, um, enjoy yourself'. Henry used wartime newsreel cinemas in Sydney and Melbourne for his own purposes. Asked how he knew that the other men in the cinema were same-sex attracted, Henry explained:

> there were small theatrettes through the city where you could go and watch newsreel and that was where other homosexuals like me would meet each other and probably for me that was the main way of meeting. You'd go into a darkened cinema, I think it still goes on, where you, sort of feel a knee come close to you and then you get up and go out and they'd get up and follow at a short period, so you weren't noticed...but it worked extremely well in those theatrettes, the news theatrettes because they're, they didn't, their lights didn't go up at all until they were finished for the day. It ran all the way through, so you could get up and go whenever you felt like it.

However, sex did not take place in the cinema.

> D: Yes. So, were the men having sex in the cinema?
>
> H: Oh no, no!
>
> D: Where did you go to have sex then?
>
> H: Um, once you got outside, and saw your, who it was that got up, it was a case of you sort of deciding whether you liked the person or not...and, ah, you would go to the nearest ah, public toilet. But most of the, most of the, those cinemas had toilets anyway. You could...go into there.

These cinemas also functioned as places to meet others who were seeking homosexual contact and sometimes facilitated the forming of relationships or friendships. Importantly, those friendships could flourish within the 'normal' heterosexual world without the circumstances or nature of the friendship being revealed. Henry recounted one such instance:

> D: Can I ask, during that whole period, so the research period, did anyone else know that you were gay? Or you kept it completely secret? You never told anyone?
>
> H: No, well, yes, yes. No, no, I mean, now I'll tell you, tell something, when I met the guy that I came down to Melbourne with ah, in a cinema...like that, and we sort of liked each other immediately. We saw, we continued the friendship or, or started the friendship and when we decided that we wanted to leave our homes 'cause he lived at home, the same as I did, and we decided, I mean I'd been to Melbourne and I knew, I had family down here, um, my mother's brother and his wife lived down here, so that was one place that we could go and stay for holidays and that.

For some men, therefore, beats became more than just a space for sex. Prior to his arrest for soliciting, Herbert, 81, enjoyed going to beats because he found them exciting and could meet others like himself. He recalled that 'it was so easy and so natural [for] two people to meet'. Beats could also be much more of a social leveller, erasing the professional/working class divide of the bars. He recounted how sex at beats meant that you could 'rub shoulders, literally, with well-known solicitors and business people' you had met the night before at a heterosexual 'social do':

> You were with your girlfriend dancing, ah, it is the crème de la crème of guests ... you go to a urinal, guess what, somebody who you had met there, is at that party and thank you very much, they would like to have sex with you too!

Many same-sex attracted men outwardly 'passed' by having girlfriends and attending heterosexual social functions. But these same men also indulged in clandestine homosexual liaisons to satisfy homosexual desire. Herbert also recalled that, despite the anonymous nature of beats, there was occasionally a sense of community, especially when he was younger. He remembered one evening in particular when he went to a beat in St Kilda: 'which I might add, I didn't know at the time, was very famous'. When his car wouldn't start, he went back into the public toilet and asked for help. 'I said, "Hi you guys" and they all came out and pushed me down the street!' Herbert thought it was all 'hysterical!' The incident was significant for Herbert because he 'learned that that was a healthy situation of gay life and also of a unity'.

Uninhibited sex: Henry's story (continued), Arthur's story (continued), Tristan's story (continued), Norman's story (continued)

The clandestine nature of illicit homosexual sex meant that its location and practice remained largely hidden from the heterosexual world and also eluded many homosexuals. Willett observed: 'homosexuals created spaces for themselves outside what was publicly permitted and forbidden, catalogued and described'.[22] Ironically, homosexual 'spaces' were possible because homosexuality was silenced. Censorship of sexuality itself created a certain freedom for homosexuals to search for sex, because it was considered impolite to even discuss the topic in public.

For homosexuals who were able to build knowledge, most often through personal contacts, a fun and lively homosexual sex life was possible. This group comprised those who had a much more robust, developed sense of their sexuality and who used knowledge to their own advantage. Often, this growth meant that men 'graduated' from beats to finding sex in settings that were previously unavailable to them. Opportunities for sex and for enjoying its emotional connections presented more readily because these men regularly mixed with other homosexuals and, consequently, socialised in places where sex could be initiated or take place. Some of the men in this grouping also visited beats, but many did not need to; they could find sex at private parties or organise liaisons while at homosexual gatherings in hotels. Questioned about how he found sex once the wartime cinemas no longer operated, Henry, 95, answered that it was 'usually at parties' in private houses, where the guests were all homosexual and 'mostly all men'. Asked whether they were fun, Henry chuckled knowingly and replied: 'Of course they were fun! You made a lot of friends that way too, not necessarily sexually'. Henry recalled that, although sex occurred at the parties, 'mostly it wasn't at the party' because 'you either met somebody and you made arrangements to meet – and that's the way it went on'. Sex could be more than a physical release. Often, it provided a backdrop for men learning about themselves and creating friendships with other homosexuals.

Arthur, 74, also recalled sex at parties but gave a different account of how much went on. Only homosexual men were present at parties he attended; usually: 'there might be 12, 15 people or so – but obviously there would be much bigger ones, [bigger] occasions than that'. Asked what happened at the parties, Arthur self-effacingly replied: 'Well, with me absolutely nothing, unfortunately!' Pressed on whether sex occurred at parties, Arthur laughed and explained:

> Oh, of course!! Oh yes, yeah! On occasion you would walk into a bedroom and there'd be a whole group on a bed, which I always think was a bit horrifying, but anyway!

Some men enjoyed frequent sex in this way. Although there was always the possibility of police raids, these men were self-confident and uninhibited by religious or moral concerns. For men like Tristan, 81, who was unashamed of his sexuality, finding sex partners was relatively easy:

> I can remember when I was working at the Savoy Hotel, I was walking, it was, I used to work from 9 o'clock in the morning till 9 o'clock at night every day, 12 hours a day. And I remember walking down the um, the Savoy had a big, long marble hallway going back down to the Saloon Bar, and I was walking down there and said um, some bloke propositioned me for sex, and I said, 'I'm sorry, but you can't afford me!' You'd go but they, but the barmaids knew I was gay, and they didn't care you know, cause I, every time they wanted something done I would do it and um, all the rest of it. The boss didn't worry about it either. But a couple, a couple of people asked me [to have sex] but I wasn't going to, you don't play in your own workplace or anything, you know, and it was just one of those things, but it was, it was obvious to people that I was gay. But I didn't have, didn't have any, much worry with it.

Tristan approached his sexuality in a very practical way:

> You've always got to remember that sex between men has been going on since the Bible times because that's why we're written in it. 'Straight', in parenthesis, men have been known to go with gay people.

Although Tristan conceded: 'I know it was not like that for a lot of people', he was more confident, noting: 'there were certain boundaries that you didn't step over, but if you stayed within the boundaries, you could have a damn good time!'

Norman, 88, was also very comfortable being homosexual. Asked how he looked for sex, he replied that he often found partners through the theatre where he worked at the time. But, for men who were attuned to their sexuality and the possibilities of homosexual sex, opportunities presented in everyday life. When Norman was 17, around 1947:

> N: When I was first at work at the saleyards, and I used to get the train at Aspendale, Flinders Street, Flinders Street to Flemington...6 o'clock in the morning and go out there. Coming home it could be midnight, the last train. One night on the, it must have been the last train, the door just opened as it was about to leave and this bloke sat opposite me and talking about being, going to the Army and Navy Club, and what he saw in the toilet there and all of a sudden, he's on his knees, and of course I was... quite happy to be relieved!
>
> D: Mmm, and they didn't have cameras in those days!
>
> N: No, they didn't, and it was between Flinders Street and Richmond!

Norman also recalled a visit to the cinema:

> to see *'Mildred Pierce'*... in the city. Monday was my day off and I used to get dressed up and go to town and see two films, and I'm sitting there, one in from the aisle and next to me comes a man, sits down and then, I thought he was going to sleep – he was starting to lean on me, then his hand's on my leg and the next thing my fly's undone! And ah, the lady in front had a blue rinse and [then] he disappeared!

Men on the lookout could also find sex close to home. Norman recounted another youthful sexual encounter:

> In Sydney I had a flat in King's Cross and down below there was

a delicatessen with two men, and I got the feeling they were gay and they used to chat to me and blah, blah, blah, and one of them said 'Oh, we're just around the corner, come over and have a coffee' sort of thing, so he was on his own and the next thing it was real sex and that became a fairly regular thing.

Meanings of sex: Spencer's story (continued), Barry's story (continued), Tristan's story (continued)

According to Dowsett, a sociology of sexuality needs to do more than just describe sex acts; it must also look deeper into their meanings. He maintains that it is incumbent on us to seek to understand: 'the circumstances, their emotional and relational context, the significance of the events, and the fantasies behind them'.[23] For the men contributing to this book, sex was not just a desire for physical release. It also involved a deep longing to offer and receive affection and to enjoy physical bodily contact without necessarily needing to be overly sexually stimulated. It was also about what Bersani calls 'sexual sociability', which he differentiates from 'sociability' because it 'brings bodies together'.[24] Lack of opportunities for sex created a void for many of the men as they looked for 'a sense of connectedness and a reduction in feelings of isolation and loneliness'.[25]

Possibilities for this homosexual connectedness in the 1940s and 1950s were especially spasmodic and fragile for some men. Homosexual desire was directly linked to shame and fear, which in turn created 'self-doubt, sometimes self-loathing, which often caused considerable psychological damage'.[26] Nigel, 74, was quite clear in his teenage years that he wanted homosexual sex but did not act on his desire because of the 'inhibitions...[of] religion'. Donald, 77, recalled feeling 'dirty' after engaging in homosexual sex, because he knew that 'society didn't approve' and that homosexuality was thought to 'be unnatural'.

Spencer, 74, recalled his confusion as a teenager about what was expected of him and why he didn't seem capable of behaving like other boys. He felt alienated and concerned that there was something fundamentally wrong with him:

> I was very aware all the time I was sort of looking at men's legs or ah, around puberty, just before or around puberty I'd had sexual experiences with boys. So, there were sexual, but I always thought in my mind though, it was just puberty.

One particular homosexual experience occurred when Spencer was 16. It remains in his memory because it was a sudden and shocking revelation that his whole world was not as it had seemed. Although 'hardly anything happened', the encounter shook him to his core because: 'I thought then, "Oh my God! What's wrong with me?! This is weird!"'. He 'felt pretty guilty and pretty confused about it', and this reaction took on even deeper meanings for him five years later:

> D: So, you felt a lot of guilt about the homosexual sex?
>
> S: Yeah, that one, yes, I did. In fact, there was, I was telling someone yesterday, I'm wondering whether I'd tell you this, but I've never even really told anybody, not that I'm ashamed of it but...the sexual experience happened out on a sheep station where his family lived. I stayed with family friends on the sheep station for a few weeks and had a very brief sexual experience. I think only one, maybe a couple of times, going into, into the car and playing with each other.
> I'm not really sure if there was orgasm or anything. I don't remember, but he was a very macho, little wiry little guy called 'Jockey', a lovely young man, but very sort of closed up Australian...And at 21 he drove himself at very high speed into a tree and killed himself I heard later, through the family friends, you know. I always felt, not guilty, but very concerned that, certainly once I came out [as homosexual], much, much, much later, I often thought maybe I could have helped him. But of course...I was in no position at all.

Homosexual sex connected with experiences of desire, pleasure, guilt, death and suicide. It is unsurprising that its meanings for Spencer were complex and impenetrable.

Similarly, the little knowledge Barry, 80, had of homosexual sex as a young adult meant that his first homosexual experience created a complex mix of emotions, even as he participated:

> I knew by the fact that it was two men engaging in sex – that I was engaged in sex with another man, and that it was behind closed doors of course, that there was something not 'normal' about it and therefore I soon learned, it was something furtive, as I say 'furtive', is the word – not to be spoken of, nobody was to know.

Despite the range of their sexual experiences, however, the interviewed men talked of homosexual sex as a revelation, as something they desired and wanted to experience more. Although being homosexual was problematic for most, homosexual sex was almost universally liberating and pleasurable – if often followed by psychological distress. The intimacy of sex and its connecting of the physical and the emotional had the power to free men from their psychological demons, if only for short periods of time. Barry described his first homosexual sex, in 1956, as an almost romantic and revelatory experience:

> D: How old were you when you discovered what it [homosexuality] was all about?
>
> B: Oh, I can tell you exactly – I was 19.
>
> D: And how do you know that?
>
> B: Oh, because I lost my virginity! At the Mission to Seamen!
>
> D: Oh, that's a very nice place to lose it!
>
> B: A combination of gin and Rachmaninov! And...suddenly everything opened up that night. I realised that that was me, this was now an established fact about me and my whole future. And that my whole future took on a new vista...a scary vista, scary because I knew that it had to be secret.

The Mission to the Seamen, where 'I lost my virginity... and my whole future took on a new vista'. (Barry)

This interview exchange with Barry highlights the links between the physical sex he had and its emotional and psychological meanings. The fact that he still vividly recalls the event, over 60 years later, attests to the significance of his first homosexual sex. Barry described this evening of sex as the moment he understood what homosexuality would mean for him. Physical intimacy with another man brought physical and emotional pleasure; but it also instilled knowledge about who Barry was, what he wanted, whom he wanted to be with, and how this would impact the way he lived his life. Further, this sex partner introduced Barry for the first time to the concept of homosexual culture by recommending:

> a number of forbidden books [and] novels... all of them banned you know... I knew then that it was against the law 'cause he told me it was against the law to have these books in one's possession – so, I wanted them!... I remember getting a copy of a rare, privately printed English translation of *Our Lady of the Flowers*, Jean Genet you know, it was just a mind-blowing book.[27]

Suddenly, Barry's understanding that 'relationships with human beings was that between men and women' as the 'normal' state was less clear and open to question. This impacted profoundly on him and the belief systems he had developed as a minister of the church.

Tristan, 81, had a more hedonistic view of homosexual sex and did not suffer from mental anguish when engaging in it. Sexuality was a positive force that allowed him to enjoy his life and make the most of it, despite the illegal nature of homosexual sex at the time. His description of one particularly fond memory illustrated his pragmatic approach to sexuality:

> You would go to a party and then you might meet somebody there at the party and then you would go home with them, you know, but sex was always there – you never went without! And you've got to remember, nothing could hurt you! You know, so back in 1958, '59 you were absolutely beautiful! And you were immortal! I was blonde and fair and slim. God, when I look at some of the photos of those days, hell's bells! I finished up one night with a about six-foot-six guardsman, one of those fellows that wears those big hats, you know? And he wanted me! I was going to be his, there was going to be nobody else who was going to get me! I thought 'Ok' and he was lovely!...But oh God! All the way in [to the city] we had to drive him back to the ship, the next morning that they were on...one of those Grenadier Guards, or the Marines, one of those. And all I can remember, when we were going back and he was cuddling me in the back seat of a car, and all I can remember is his thick heavy red jacket that was giving me almost beard rash on my face! But he was a lovely man you know, and that's the way you'd do it. You know well, that's, sometimes you thought, well this big guy, I'm quite sure he would probably go home to a girlfriend. I'm quite sure he did, but he enjoyed, I know he enjoyed me because of the way he made me feel...he said 'Oh, God, I wish you were living in Britain!' Look, there was always sex if you wanted it!

Tristan accounted for his homosexuality in a less philosophical or existential way than many others. He did not struggle with moral concerns. He found meaning in the joy of homosexual sex and the emotional, human connections it afforded him. His ability to find such affirmation in sex with men created a sense of wellbeing that eluded the majority of those contributing to this book. In stark contrast to many others, he described the postwar years as:

> probably one of the best times...because you were young... and when you're young you just go for it! You know, there's no holding you back, even though it was, you had to, it was a clandestine sort of thing, it still didn't matter.

His recollections of the search for sex are important. They offer evidence that it was possible to embrace one's homosexuality and to explore its pleasures in 1940s and 1950s Australia, provided this occurred away from heterosexual scrutiny. Men like Tristan, who secretly rejected the cultural norms he was expected to follow, were already challenging generally accepted views of homosexuality as deviant and immoral. He was not alone, as another of his entertaining anecdotes reveals:

> You were never brazen [though] there was one, you might not be able to put this in your [thesis] paper, but there was one bloke we knew that would walk around and sort of say, he'd meet some young bloke and say, 'Do you fuck?' [and] he very seldom got knocked back! There was no Grindr or anything like that. It was just verbal and eye contact and a smile. It was like a sort of a magic period or something...everybody knew what they were there for!

'Magic period' succinctly repositions the 1940s and 1950s as far from 'dreary and intolerant' for those homosexuals who refused to allow heteronormatively constructed beliefs and laws to define who they were or what they could be.[28]

Embracing homosexual

The narratives of the men contributing to this book illustrate an acknowledgement of a deep sexual longing and a willingness to satisfy it, even if this involved danger, guilt or confusion. These men were courageous. Their determination to satisfy their homosexual desire challenged myths about their sexuality and circumvented laws that made it illegal. Engaging in homosexual sex forced an acknowledgement of difference and initiated a redefining of the self and its place in heterosexual society. Often, the process of redefinition was frightening and nebulous. It also precipitated a recognition that life would need to be lived avoiding public or family scrutiny – necessitating changes in relationships and the flow of information between parents, work colleagues or heterosexual friends.

Knowledge lies in explaining 'the shaping or limiting of choice and action and the resistance to that constraint'.[29] The participants in this book had one thing in common: they all desired homosexual sex and all looked for it. Even surreptitious homosexual sex carried deep meanings, because it was a pushback against heteronormative definitions and compulsion. What varied was their degrees of knowledge about how to find homosexual sex, opportunities to engage in it and locations to accommodate it, and its meaning. Success or otherwise most often depended on access to homosexual communities. Men in 'precarious' communities may have had limited sex because of a lack of 'space, time, interaction, relationship and of knowledge'.[30] For those with some knowledge, beats were ubiquitous and easily accessed. Sex at beats involved the danger of being bashed, the possibility of exposure through arrest and, for many men, personal moral implications from feelings of guilt and shame. For some, beats were erotic; their dangers added a sexual frisson to the experience. Sex partners could also be found in bars, but men needed knowledge of their existence, the courage to frequent them, the confidence to approach someone and a location where sex could occur without danger. Many of those who participated in the bar culture discovered that its sociability opened doors to private parties and, therefore, an expansion of homosexual contacts and cultural intelligence – although not all who visited bars were able to fully harness the networking it afforded. Private parties also required knowledge, contacts and the good fortune of being invited. For those men who 'broke the code' into this homosexual underworld, the rewards included a fun social life and a positive affirmation of what a homosexual sexual, emotional and intellectual life could be.

Meanings of homosexual sex and men's physical, emotional and psychological responses to it were varied. All interviewees (apart from James) recorded that physical sex brought release and pleasure – and all wanted more. Conversely, emotional and psychological responses to sex were complex and much more connected to the individual's belief systems, religious background, family situation and social connections to other homosexuals (and, therefore, deeper knowledge). Many of the interviewees felt a lingering regret about sexual opportunities lost. Remarkably, in the following decades, 16 of the 27 men found stable and fulfilling sexual relationships at some point. Fifteen remain in long-term relationships now – a telling indication of these men's stoicism and ability to overcome cultural and institutional prejudice. Altman observed in 1971:

> the wonder is not how many homosexuals are neurotic but how many manage to develop happy and productive lives in the face of their repudiation of social norms.[31]

This outcome, however, took many, many years for most of the men who contributed to this book.

6

So now we know

The story of their lives

Knowledge about homosexuality – its meanings, its cultural practice, its illegality and its underworld existence – defined and separated the lived experience of homosexual men who survived and those who thrived. Individual and shared homosexual knowledge (or lack of it) dictated how homosexual men viewed themselves; how they interpreted society's view of their sexuality; how much contact they had with other homosexuals; the degree to which they lived in fear or not; how they interacted with school friends, family, and work colleagues; how and where they socialised; whom they had sex with; and where sex took place. Central to the inability of many to take full advantage of their knowledge was the lack of access to language that could describe who they were in affirming ways.

Most homosexual men recognised their difference early in school. That difference was not always framed by sexuality, but it marked them out as targets for bullying by teachers, other students and – sometimes – their own parents (usually fathers). Two main factors triggered this bullying: either the boy's mannerisms were interpreted as effeminate, or he was uninterested and unskilled in sport or other perceived 'masculine' pursuits. A few boys who were sporty avoided the torment others endured. They could 'pass' in a way that others could not. Their enjoyment of their school years completely eluded others. Often, the reasons for being labelled a 'sissy' or a 'pansy' were nebulous, particularly to the bullied boy. Even more confusing was the lack of clarity around the words' meanings and their targets. Often, boys reached early adolescence or adulthood before understanding the connections with homosexuality. The meanings of homosexuality itself were also obscure.

Family and work life for homosexuals was often not much better than at school, forcing men to have 'multiple identities' within the family, at work and with other homosexuals.[1] Parents (especially fathers) and siblings expected boys to be 'masculine' and to excel at 'masculine' activities, such as playing sport. Work colleagues later reinforced this attitude. A few mothers were supportive of their homosexual sons – always inferred, rather than articulated, with a 'don't ask, don't tell' approach. Religion magnified the negative attitudes within the home. Although ministers did not use the word 'homosexual' in churches, they made it very clear that any sex outside marriage was sinful. Homosexuals learned to fear police, who had the power to entrap, harass, bash and charge men engaged in illegal acts. Only a tiny minority of men had supportive parents and knew that their homosexuality did not threaten their relationship with their families. They rejected notions of homosexual deviancy and instead led positive, fun and sexually active homosexual lives. Instead of living with fear and shame, they maintained high levels of self-confidence and privately embraced their sexuality.

Those searching for other homosexuals often only gleaned knowledge of homosexual communities or practice from court or media reports about lewd behaviour in public places. This information at least indicated one way to find sex. Mostly, knowledge was simply passed in conversations among homosexuals who gathered together. Those who did not find communities were often left in ignorance of homosexual ways of being. Homosexual sex was available, but beats could be dangerous. Many men suffered psychological distress while accessing sex, because it was illegal and considered sinful. Despite these barriers, all of the men were adamant that they wanted homosexual sex and that they enjoyed it.

For those in the know, sex was available and all the more delightful through being covert and illegitimate. These men attended lively hotel gatherings, fabulous dinner parties, fancy dress balls and, sometimes, country picnics. Less connected homosexuals (the majority) would have been astounded to learn that such social life existed. Life could include sociability, community, fun, surreptitious gatherings, pleasure, camaraderie and sex. 'Homosexual' bars, private parties and beats provided the environments for these activities. Such connections may seem pedestrian and unremarkable now, but they were in essence the beginnings of postwar homosexual communities – although such gatherings were without any of the overtly political or cultural definitions of later movements. In a theoretical sense, the very act of gathering was a beginning point for a rethinking of what it was to be homosexual, unifying men through a sense of belonging. These men forged new and more affirming meanings of what it was to be a homosexual simply by taking the risk of being together.

Sadly, not all men were able to find the inner strength to accept their homosexuality. These interviewees were understandably reluctant to recall in any detail the men who took their own lives rather than face the humiliation of being declared a homosexual, but they did know them. We cannot know the numbers; their voices were silenced a long time ago.

The stories of those who survived refute the notion that 'modern gay identity came in the late 1960s with gay liberation'.[2] Their first-hand knowledge fills gaps in our homosexual history and quietly celebrates the men's extraordinary resilience. Importantly, the stories used here have been collected just prior to a point where they would have been lost forever. Several men have passed away since I interviewed them.

A new homosexual history

This book has aimed to uncover, describe and explain the lived experience of homosexual men in Australia from the end of World War II to the beginning of the 'Sexual Revolution' in the 1960s. I sought to understand how homosexual men in Australia survived the challenges they faced during this period. The answers to the questions are found, of course, in the personal histories of the 27 interviewees. All these men had to build and sustain a self that contravened the rules of society. In 1940s and 1950s Australia, none was able to live a life where his sexuality was openly acknowledged and accepted by (heterosexual) friends, family or work colleagues.

From a contemporary position of relative homosexual privilege, we can now feel rightfully offended by Australian society's treatment of homosexuals in the years following the war. We might rush to interpret such lived experience as wholly unsatisfactory and without joy. But such an interpretation would simply repeat past summaries of the 1940s and 1950s era as uniformly and 'appallingly repressive', and it is actually a much more nuanced and complex history.[3] At times, it is surprisingly 'gay' – in all senses of the word. Simply looking back and responding from our modern sensitivity would obscure, rather than illuminate, the past. We would relinquish an opportunity to contextualise the settings, beliefs, mores and experiences of homosexuals in navigating and surviving their same-sex attraction.

Gay and lesbian historians have traditionally drawn a distinction between 'homosexual' history and 'gay and lesbian' history as a way of marking out the era prior to 'gay liberation' and the era that followed. Denis Altman argues in 'The end of the homosexual?' that 'the early period of gay and lesbian history has been well chronicled' by authors such as Graham Willett in *Living out loud*, Denise Thompson in *Flaws in the social fabric* and Robert Reynolds in *From camp to queer*. More recently, Reynolds and Shirleene Robinson have authored *Gay and lesbian, then and now: Australian stories from a social revolution*.

The period following World War II deserves much more of our attention if we want to fully explain liberation in the late 1960s and early 1970s. Rather than being separate to an 'early' history (Altman was actually referring to a much later period, in the 1980s), the postwar period is highly significant for understanding both 'homosexual' and 'gay and lesbian' history. The two are essential for an informed and thorough interpretation. One without the other lacks integrity. Viewing the historical periods largely as separate has diminished the opportunity for learning from the perspective of the two periods and how each informs the other. Further, if the 'early period of gay and lesbian history' refers to the beginning of liberation history from the late 1960s and early 1970s, then such dating is insufficient to allow a holistic view of either 'homosexual' or 'gay and lesbian' history; it has, therefore, not been as 'well chronicled' as Altman suggests.

Altman also wrote about 'the new identity politics' that arose from the late 1960s and the ways in which gay liberation aimed to 'understand why homosexuals were stigmatised, why they were oppressed and how to fight that oppression'. He discusses an emerging, self-confident, positive sense of homosexual identity formation that rejected the old 'failed identification' of homosexuality as being abnormal.[4] Homosexuals did not, individually or collectively, fight against homosexual oppression in the postwar years. Nevertheless, this period can help us to fully understand the origins of stigmatisation and oppression that later generations challenged.

The history of postwar homosexuality is not a militant or radical narrative. It is important because, if we are to understand gay liberation,[2] we need to firstly explain what homosexuals were being liberated from. The lived experience of homosexuals in this book can more accurately and intimately reveal how, when, where, why and by whom they were stigmatised and oppressed. Importantly, their stories can explain how they interpreted stigmatisation and oppression. They also shed light on how some of the men overcame such hurdles, while others could not. Whether that struggle was won or lost, all were impacted in some way or other.

The stories of their survival lay claim to a revision of history that confronts the complexities of radical changes in beliefs, culture and social relations over the seven decades since. They are a revisiting and a renegotiation of meanings from 70 years ago through a different, more liberated, more educated and more accepting lens. If the 1960s are connected to the sexual revolution, the 1970s to gay liberation, the 1980s and early 1990s to confronting AIDS and the 2000s perhaps to inclusivity, then the 1940s and 1950s emerge from these stories as an era of homosexual survival and the construction of its meanings by powerful societal institutions on the one hand, and homosexual men themselves on the other.

Group recollection of what it meant to 'be' homosexual in 1940s and 1950s Australia permits us to reassess the meanings of the 'early period'. In the process, perhaps homosexual history becomes less self-assured; at the same time, it is enriched. It offers a more authentic, experience-based account of itself and challenges the ideas that this history has been adequately expounded or that we can better understand this history by splitting it into two separate eras. Instead, by rigorously examining the period prior to sexual liberation, we can more comprehensively situate what came later. New knowledge can emerge, where meaning is derived from the interpretation of stories. But if we have not issued an invitation for those stories to be told, if we have not offered to listen, if we have not contemplated their meanings and framed their historical significance, then our understanding of what came after will be impoverished. By developing a fuller understanding of what life was like for homosexuals in the 1940s and 1950s, we can more accurately comprehend the precursors and push factors that later led to individual voices and movements that agitated for change. That they were oppressed is not new. But their stories go beyond descriptions of oppression and address what men thought about it, how they managed their lives while accommodating it, and what impacts this struggle had on them.

This new homosexual history ducks and weaves and infiltrates its way through Australian mainstream history. These stories of rejection and sexual otherness challenge our sense of ourselves as an egalitarian, inclusive country. Stories that show the ability of a maligned minority to defy repressive laws and beliefs and to create spaces that permitted their self-expression attract our admiration. Legal and moral barriers created to silence homosexuals ironically energised them to seek out ways to circumvent their impacts.

There is no single narrative that represents the lives of the 27 men in this book. The pathways and experiences available to them differed.

Determining factors included knowledge of homosexuality; emotional and intellectual responses to being homosexual; personal agency; family attitudes to homosexuality; religious practice; workplace environment; contact with doctors, ministers of religion or police; personal responses to homosexual desire; and access to homosexual communities and sex. Together, these narratives provide rich and complex detail. They have a visceral impact and a rawness. They reveal humility, a startling frankness, and individual and group resilience. This lived experience becomes much more than stories; the tellers are also challenging history and societal power structures to confess and confront their deliberate omissions. They force us to confront new, uncomfortable knowledge that disrupts our preferred version of history. This opens new possibilities for recognition, reparation, expunging criminal records and committing as a society to confront past transgressions and not to repeat them.

In *Living out loud*, Graham Willett argues that contemporary acceptance of homosexuality, and indeed other sexualities, has occurred because 'institutions and structures have proved very much more adaptable than expected'.[5] In the 1940s and 1950s, such change was not anticipated at all, because homosexuality was so external to the norm. Yet, this is a further connection between our past and present: the homosexual men of the period found spaces where they could be whomever they wanted to be, if only at certain times and in certain environments.

This struggle to survive has always been a common thread running through homosexual history. Three important dimensions help us to understand the lives of homosexual men in the 1940s and 1950s – and the import of those lives on the contemporary position of homosexuals in society. Firstly, if the notion of 'living out loud' can be described as modern homosexuals shouting (about gay rights, law reform, discrimination and visibility), the opposite is true postwar. Silence regulated homosexual lives. Heteronormative culture and laws disparaged homosexuality through social institutions, including schools, families, churches, courts, medicine and marriage. Mothers, but more particularly fathers and brothers; school children and teachers; governments; employers and work colleagues; doctors and psychiatrists; police, lawyers and judges; ministers of religion; and the media all conveyed this condemnation. Homosexuals struggled to define who and what they were, how they could live their lives, and who could and could not share in their knowledge of difference. Vilification of homosexuals induced suffering, self-doubt, secrecy, shame and fear. Breaking the silence – being caught at a beat, for example – publicly exposed homosexual existence and challenged prevailing social and moral norms. Shaming, loss of employment and loss of family were the risks.

A second dimension of homosexual lives was the need to organise around heteronormative behavioural expectations. Homosexuals who were unable to find ways to do this often suffered physical or mental abuse, particularly at school and within families. Effeminacy, or simply being labelled as effeminate, was nebulously connected with homosexuality and made suspect men an easy target. A lack of sexual interest in women or insufficient enthusiasm for 'masculine' pastimes created suspicion. Marriage was expected, and homosexuals required ingenuity in order to avoid it. Secrecy around repressed homosexual desire often led to failed marriages, damaged relationships with parents and psychological distress. Even so, and contrary to past assumptions, many homosexuals remained single.

Yet, this is not the whole story. A third dimension of this history records that a significant number of homosexual men went beyond an accommodation of heterosexual society. These men carefully but enthusiastically worked out ways to thrive within the boundaries of heterosexual absolutism. Instead of being restricted by, or fearful of, their homosexuality, they embraced it. They used heteronormative rules cunningly, not as a measure of what they could not do, but as a means for defining what they could do. Despite restrictions on their public lives, in private (usually in bars and at private parties) they 'had a ball' and revelled in the knowledge that most in heterosexual society were ignorant of their lifestyle. They nurtured their homosexual networks, so many spent most of their social life only within those circles. Life was far from dreary, boring or fearful. Indeed, in contrast to strict moral regulation around heterosexual sex during the postwar years, these homosexual men enjoyed as much sex as they desired, without any of the moral scruples that heterosexuals faced. This created a level of sexual freedom unimagined by heterosexual (and sections of homosexual) society. The thrivers constructed a platform for the reimagining and redefining of what it was to be homosexual. Postwar Australian homosexual history therefore has a more clandestinely colourful and life-affirming character than previously thought. Thrivers didn't miss the party; they just didn't invite the rest of society!

There are still limitations to our understanding of this history. Minority group experience within homosexual history of the period has the capacity to reveal important insights, but it remains unheard. However, it was overwhelmingly middle class white men who were willing to tell their stories for this book – perhaps because they had benefited most from the new freedoms brought by gay liberation. This omission of the experience of 'the other' from within the homosexual minority population points to a silence that highlights critical lost or unrecovered historical knowledge.

A second caution in oral history is the memory reliability of interviewees. This was particularly relevant for this book because of the advanced ages of the men. Memories of events and experiences of 70 years ago may not be accurate. However, this book is not about finding absolute 'truth' around homosexual men's lives. Rather, it aims to relive the past through their memories and emotions. It is not concerned with the accuracy of minute detail. Even if storytellers fall into repeating mythologies, those mythologies and their interpretations help us to learn more about the way people constructed their lives and how society reacted to those constructions.[6] They advance our knowledge while also permitting us to form new questions.

Plummer points out: 'stories help people to say certain things at certain times and in certain places, and likewise not to say them at others'.[7] *Now* is the time for these stories to be told. They provide us with a focal point from which to review Australia's responses to homosexuality and the impacts it has had on Australian lives. Changes in attitudes to sexuality also reveal progress in Australia.[8] In the end, what matters is that the stories are told and the memories shared; in the telling, that silenced history is 'unsilenced'. One participant remarked at the end of his interview that he wanted his story told because he 'didn't want it untold'.

A postscript to our future

One of the earliest interviews conducted for this book was with George, who was 87. He recounted a lifetime of guilt and shame because of his homosexuality. But, decades after that era, George progressively recast his sense of homosexual self. He is now bursting with a sense of freedom, happiness and sexual openness. He concluded his interview by declaring: *'I am me! Here I am!'* This provided the launching point for these stories and their offering to homosexual history. They reveal a new history that helps us to bridge the gaps in our imagining of the homosexual experience in Australia. They tell us about hardship, censorship, prejudice, fear, shame and isolation – but they also reveal resourcefulness, sexual freedom, homosexual sociability and self-determination. Their histories invite us to celebrate George's joy. We can now approach that history from a privileged position of knowledge about where our homosexual elders came from. We celebrate their histories, because they gift to us our future.

Vale to those who have passed away since the recording of their interviews.

Endnotes

Chapter 1

1. J. Weeks, 'Queer(y)ing the "Modern Homosexual"', *Journal of British Studies*, vol. 51, no. 3, 2012, p. 529.

2. A. Katz, *Gay American History: Lesbians and Gay Men In the U.S.A. A Documentary*, Crowell, 1976, p. 1.

3. D. Altman, *Homosexual: Oppression & Liberation*, University of Queensland Press, 2012, p. 45.

4. D. Altman, *End of the Homosexual?*, University of Queensland Press, 2013, p. 70.

5. W. Murdoch, *Kamp Melbourne in the 1920s and & '30s: Trade, Queans and Inverts*, Cambridge Scholars Publishing, 2017, pp. 3, 182.

6. R. Aldrich, *Colonialism and Homosexuality*, Routledge, 2003, p. 224.

7. G. Carbery, *Towards Homosexual Equality in Australian Criminal Law – a Brief History*, Australian Lesbian & Gay Archives (Australian Queer Archives), 1993, pp. 2, 53.

8. 'Police discover pervert haunt', *Brisbane Telegraph*, 24 June 1953, p. 3.

9. Victorian Bar, 'Obituary – The Hon John Joseph Hedigan QC', 2016, https://www.Vicbar.Com.Au/News-Events/Obituary-Hon-John-Joseph-Hedigan-QC, accessed 19 Aug 2019.

10. Marypana, 'The "Detestable and Abominable Vice" – the 1533 Act.' Pre-Elizabethan England, retrieved 12 (Wilkens, 2015), 2012, pre-elizabethanengland.blogspot.com/2012/05/detestable-and-abominable-Vice-1533-Act.html, accessed 3 Jan 2022.

11 Reserve Bank of Australia, https://www.rba.gov.au/calculator/annualPreDecimal.html.

12 C. Rasmussen, 'Medicine', *The Encyclopedia of Women & Leadership in Twentieth-Century Australia*, https://www.Womenaustralia.Info/Leaders/Biogs/Wle0133b.htm, accessed 25 May 2022.

13 D. M. Dunlop, S. Alstead & A. G. Macgregor (eds.), *Textbook of Medical Treatment*, E. & S. Livingstone, 1968, p. 433.

14 A. P. Noyes, preface to *Modern Clinical Psychology*, W. B. Saunders Company, 1948. A. P. Noyes, Modern Clinical Psychiatry 3rd edn, W. B. Saunders Co., 1948.

15 Dunlop, Alstead & Macgregor, *Textbook of Medical Treatment*, p. 432.

16 A. P. Noyes & L. C. Kolb, 'Paranoia and Paranoid Conditions' in *Modern Clinical Psychology*, W. B. Saunders Company, 1948, p. 401.

17 R. Liddicoat, 'Homosexuality', *South African Journal of Science*, May 1962, p. 145.

18 H. Sutton, 'The Problem of Homosexuality', *Sydney Morning Herald*, 5 Dec 1953, p. 2.

Chapter 2

1 R. Croome, 'Australia's Homophobia Is Deeply Rooted in Its Colonial Past', *The Guardian Online*, 30 September 2017.

2 M. Bull, S. Pinto & P. Wilson, 1991, 'Homosexual Law Reform in Australia', *Trends & Issues in Crime and Criminal Justice*, no. 29.

3 E. Henderson, 'Of Signifiers and Sodomy: Privacy, Public Morality and Sex in the Decriminalisation Debates', *Melbourne University Law Review*, vol. 20, no. 4, p. 1024.

4 A. Kaladelfos, 'The "Greatest Menace": The Unexpected Outcomes of Policing Homosexuality', *Australian Women's History Network*, http://www.auswhn.org.au/blog/policing-homosexuality/, 24 Sep 2017.

5 State apology to those convicted under unjust laws against homosexual acts – Premier's speech, 24 May 2016, https://www.premier.vic.gov.au/state-apology-those-convicted-under-unjust-laws-against-homosexual-acts-premiers-speech.

6   Henderson, 'Of Signifiers and Sodomy', p. 1024.
7   Kaladelfos, 'The "Greatest Menace"'.
8   'Police discover pervert haunt', *Brisbane Telegraph*, 24 June 1953, p. 3.
9   Victorian Bar, 'Obituary – The Hon John Joseph Hedigan QC', 2016, https://www.Vicbar.Com.Au/News-Events/Obituary-Hon-John-Joseph-Hedigan-QC, accessed 19 Aug 2019.
10 Marypana, 'The "Detestable and Abominable Vice" – the 1533 Act.' Pre-Elizabethan England, retrieved 12 (Wilkens, 2015), 2012, pre-elizabethanengland.blogspot.com/2012/05/detestable-and-abominable-Vice-1533-Act.html, accessed 3 Jan 2022.
11 Reserve Bank of Australia, https://www.rba.gov.au/calculator/annualPreDecimal.html.
12 C. Rasmussen, 'Medicine', *The Encyclopedia of Women & Leadership in Twentieth-Century Australia*, https://www.Womenaustralia.Info/Leaders/Biogs/Wle0133b.htm, accessed 25 May 2022.
13 D. M. Dunlop, S. Alstead & A. G. Macgregor (eds.), *Textbook of Medical Treatment*, E. & S. Livingstone, 1968, p. 433.
14 A. P. Noyes, preface to *Modern Clinical Psychology*, W. B. Saunders Company, 1948. A. P. Noyes, *Modern Clinical Psychiatry* 3rd edn, W. B. Saunders Co., 1948.
15 Dunlop, Alstead & Macgregor, *Textbook of Medical Treatment*, p. 432.
16 A. P. Noyes & L. C. Kolb, 'Paranoia and Paranoid Conditions' in *Modern Clinical Psychology*, W. B. Saunders Company, 1948, p. 401.
17 R. Liddicoat, 'Homosexuality', *South African Journal of Science*, May 1962, p. 145.
18 H. Sutton, 'The Problem of Homosexuality', *Sydney Morning Herald*, 5 Dec 1953, p. 2.

Chapter 3

1   C. Nelson & M. Martin, *Sexual Pedagogies: Sex Education in Britain, Australia, and America, 1879–2000*, Pan Macmillan, 2004, p. 87.
2   Nelson & Martin, p. 87.

3   Nelson & Martin, p. 90.

4   L. Segal, *Slow Motion: Changing Masculinities, Changing Men*, Palgrave Macmillan, 2007, p. 13.

5   T. Gray, *Ode on a Distant Prospect of Eton College Oxford*, Clarendon Press, 1924.

6   C. Belfrage, *The American Inquisition, 1945–1960: A profile of the 'McCarthy era'*, Thunder's Mouth Press, 1989. During the 1950s, Senator Joseph McCarthy of Wisconsin, USA, set out to purge the federal government of communists and subversive agents – which led to the demonisation of homosexuals.

7   Altman, *Homosexual: Oppression & Liberation*, pp. 21, 40.

8   Cited in R. Reynolds, *From Camp To Queer: Re-Making the Australian Homosexual*, Melbourne University Press, 2002, p. 96.

9   E. F. Griffith, 'Emotional Development', in E. F. Griffith (ed.), *The Road To Maturity*, Gollancz, 1944.

Chapter 4

1   A. P. Elkin, *Changes That Are Upon Us*, self-published, 1943, pp. 17, 21.

2   M. Poole, *Family: Changing Families, Changing Times*, Allen & Unwin, 2005, p. 5.

3   L. Davidoff, *The Family Story: Blood, Contract, and Intimacy 1830–1960*, Longman, 1999, p. 248.

4   D. Dempsey & J. Lindsay, *Families, Relationships and Intimate Life*, Oxford University Press, 2014, p. 20; Davidoff, The Family Story, p. 244.

5   Davidoff, *The Family Story*, pp. 244, 247.

6   M. Gilding, *The Making and Breaking of the Australian Family*, Allen & Unwin, 1991, p. 121.

7   Davidoff, *The Family Story*, p. 245.

8   M. Kirby, *A Private Life: Fragments, Memories, Friends*, Allen & Unwin, 2011, p. 29.

9   Davidoff, *The Family Story*, p. 245.

10 D. Cohen, *Family Secrets: Living With Shame From the Victorians To the Present Day*, Viking, 2013, p. 150.

11 New Zealand crime writer and theatre director (1895–1982). Accounts of her lesbianism are contested.

12 A. Murphy, *Imagining the Fifties: Private Sentiment and Political Culture In Menzies' Australia*, UNSW Press, 2000, p. 56.

13 D. Gittins, *The Family In Question, Women In Society series*, Macmillan, 1993, p. 148.

14 Dempsey & Lindsay, *Families, Relationships and Intimate Life*, p. 22.

15 A. Crossman, 'The Definition of Marriage In Sociology', *Thoughtco*, updated 1 Nov 2019.

16 S. Sarantakos, *Social Research*, Macmillan Education Australia, 1998, p. 122.

17 G. P. Murdock, *Social Structure*, Macmillan, 1949, p. 261.

18 W. Coughlan, *'Marriage Breakdown', Changes That Are Upon Us*, The University of Sydney, 1957, p. 144.

19 A. P. Elkin, *Marriage and the Family in Australia*, Angus & Robertson, 1957, p. 215.

20 Gittins, *The Family In Question*, p. 2.

21 Kirby, *A Private Life*, p. 29.

22 B. Powell, *Counted Out: Same-Sex Relations and Americans' Definitions of Family*, Russell Sage Foundation, 2010, p. 5.

23 D. Gittins, *The Family in Question*, p. 2; D. Berkowitz, 'Theorizing Lesbian and Gay Parenting: Past, Present, and Future Scholarship', *Journal of Family Theory & Review*, issue 13, 2009, p. 117.

24 B. Powell, *Counted Out*, p. 5; D. H. Demo & K. Allen, 'Diversity within Lesbian and Gay Families: Challenges and Implications for Family Theory and Research', *Journal of Social and Personal Relationships*, vol. 13. no. 3, 1996, p. 415.

25 H. McQueen, *Social Sketches of Australia*, University of Queensland, 2004, p. 186.

Chapter 5

1. J. Weeks, *Sexuality*, Taylor and Francis, 2003, p. 80.
2. G. Willett, *Living Out Loud: A History of Gay and Lesbian Activism in Australia*, Allen & Unwin, 2000, p. 196.
3. C. Warren, *Identity and Community in the Gay World*, 1974, New York, John Wiley & Sons, p. 13.
4. A. Nagle, *What Is a Community?*, Britannica Educational Publishing in association with the Rosen Publishing Group, 2018, pp. 4–9, 5.
5. Altman, *Homosexual: Oppression & Liberation*, p. 29.
6. G. Simmel, 'The Sociology of Sociability', *American Journal of Sociology*, vol. 55, no. 3, 1949, p. 255; L. Bersani, 2002, 'Sociability and Cruising', *Australian and New Zealand Journal of Art*, issue 31, 2002, p. 13.
7. A. Hyslop, Myer Elcon (1875–1938), *Australian Dictionary of Biography*, https://adb.anu.edu.au/biography/myer-elcon-7813, accessed 6 Jun 2021.
8. For further information on Lesley Walford: https://sydneylivingmuseums.com.au/documenting-nsw-homes/leslie-walford's-penthouse.
9. Warren, *Identity and Community in the Gay World*, pp. 66, 162–3.
10. Bersani, 2002, 'Sociability and Cruising', p. 14.
11. Warren, *Identity and Community in the Gay World*, p. 17.
12. C. A. Spicer, 'Australia Hotel', Melbourne the City Past & Present, https://www.emelbourne.net.au/biogs/EM00109b.htm, 2008, accessed 14 October 2020.
13. A. Murphy, *Imagining the Fifties: Private Sentiment and Political Culture in Menzies' Australia*, UNSW Press, 2000, p. 222.
14. G. Willett, 'The Darkest Decade: Homophobia in 1950s Australia', *Australian Historical Studies*, vol. 28, no. 109, 1997, p. 130.
15. D. Reeves, 'Liquor, Temperance and Legislation: The Origins of Six O'clock Closing In Victoria During WWI', https://www.Parliament.Vic.Gov.Au/Publications/Research-Papers/Send/36-Research-Papers/13740-2016-2-Liquorlaws-Hn, accessed 28 November 2017.

16 A. O'Connell, 'The Clubs with No Beer. Melbourne's 1950s Nightclubs', https://meandmybigmouth.com.au/nightclubs-melbourne-1950s/, accessed 10 June 2019.

17 Murphy, *Imagining the Fifties*, p. 56.

18 Weeks, *Sexuality*, p. 19.

19 D. Dalton, 'Gay Male Resistance In 'Beat' Spaces in Australia: A Study of Outlaw Desire', *Australian Feminist Law Journal*, 28 June 2008, p. 98.

20 R. Ford, '"Filthy, Obscene and Mad": Engendering "Homophobia"' in S. Robinson, *Homophobia: An Australian History*, The Federation Press, 2008, p. 88.

21 J. Weeks, *Sex, Politics and Society: The Regulations of Sexuality Since 1800*, Routledge, 2014, p. 2.

22 Willett, 'The Darkest Decade', p. 125.

23 G. Dowsett, *Practicing Desire: Homosexual Sex in the Era of Aids*, Stanford University Press, 1996, p. 42, p. 41.

24 Bersani, 'Sociability and Cruising', p. 28.

25 J. Wilkens, 'Loneliness and Belongingness in Older Lesbians: The Role of Social Groups As "Community"', *Journal of Lesbian Studies*, no. 191, 2015, p. 95.

26 Altman, *End of the Homosexual?*, p. 23.

27 A. Genet, *Our Lady of the Flowers*, Grove Press, 1963.

28 Murphy, *Imagining the Fifties*, p. 222.

28 Dowsett, *Practicing Desire*, p. 41.

30 Warren, *Identity and Community in the Gay World*, p. 14.

31 Altman, *Homosexual: Oppression & Liberation*, 1971, p. 28.

Chapter 6

1 R. Reynolds, 'Queer Histories'. *Creating Australia: Changing Australian History*, Allen & Unwin, 1997, p. 53.

2 Murdoch, *Kamp Melbourne in the 1920s and & '30*, p. 7.

3. G. Bedell, 'Coming Out of the Dark Ages', *The Guardian*, 24 June 2007.
4. Altman, *Homosexual: Oppression & Liberation*, 2012, p. 7.
5. Willett, *Living Out Loud*, p. 265.
6. G. Wotherspoon, *City of the Plain: History of a Gay Sub-Culture Sydney*, Hale & Iremonger, 1991, p. 31.
7. K. Plummer, *Telling Sexual Stories: Power, Change and Social World*s, Routledge, 1994, p. 172.
8. D. Altman, *End of the Homosexual?*, p. 16.

Interviewees

Ages refer to at the time of interview. Actual names are indicated in italics where permission to do so has been given. This is to facilitate any future historical research.

Arthur *(Garry Kennedy)*, 74
Arthur was born in 1944 and lives in Melbourne with his long-term male partner. He worked all his life in retail and has enjoyed socialising with many homosexual friends since his retirement. He actively supports the arts.

Barry, 80
Barry was born in 1937 and lives in Melbourne. He never married. He is a retired minister of the church. Though he has enjoyed his homosexuality at times, he also has regrets about the lack of acceptance and freedom for homosexuals in the post-war period and beyond.

Bernard *(James 'Terry' Kennedy)*, 74
Bernard was born in 1944. He was raised in country Victoria but now lives in Melbourne with his long-term male partner. He was still working until recently and had his own accountancy firm. He married once but divorced two years later. He was one of the men who represented all homosexual men at the Victorian Parliament's apology to gay men in 2017.

Colin, 80
Colin was born in 1937 and lives in country Victoria. He has been a farmer all his life but has also contributed to LGBTI organisations, particularly during

the AIDS era. He never married. He has many regrets about a life stifled by homosexual prejudice. He has never revealed his homosexuality to members of his family.

Donald, 77
Donald was born in 1940 and lives quietly in Melbourne, although he spent four years in London in the mid-1960s. He never married and had no interest in doing so. He has been constrained by his homosexuality and was the only interviewee who requested his interview not be recorded.

Douglas *(Dennis Mayall)*, 77
Douglas was born in 1937. He lives in Melbourne but also spent some years living in London. He became a department store display designer at Myer Melbourne. He never married. He has revelled in his homosexual life from the beginning. He had a 50-year relationship with his partner, who has since passed away. Douglas is out and proud and takes every opportunity to enjoy life.

Francis, 80
Francis was born in 1937 and lived in Brisbane but has now lived in Melbourne for many years. He never married. He lives with his long-term partner. He has had a varied career, including in the police, the military, trade unions, theatre and in business. His religion is very important for him. He has never allowed prejudice against homosexuality to define his life.

George *(David Morrison)*, 87
George was born in 1930 and lives in Melbourne. He was in the Air Force for over a decade before taking a teaching job in a university. He married and now has many grandchildren. Though he didn't come out until his senior years, he has loved his homosexual life and has a male partner who is in his late '80s.

Harold, 75
Harold was born in 1942 and still lives with his wife in Melbourne. They have five children and many grandchildren. He has had male partners who have lived with he and his wife. Harold began his working life in a bank and later

joined Myer department store (Melbourne) as an interior designer. He still manages his own business.

Henry *(Kendall Lovett)*, 95
Henry was born in 1922 and rose to a high level in the advertising world in Melbourne. He lived with his male partner of over 50 years. He embraced his homosexuality from a young adult age. Sadly, Henry has passed away since his interview.

Herbert, 83
Herbert was born in 1933 and lives in Melbourne. He was unsure of his career until he developed an interest in film. He then worked as a film technician. He never married. He lives with his long-term male partner. He is very grateful for the positive changes in the acceptance of homosexual people.

James, 82
James was born in 1935 and lives alone in country Victoria. He has been involved in the theatre for most of his life. He did not marry and has not had a relationship with another man, which he regrets deeply.

Lawrence, 75
Lawrence was born in 1942 in New Zealand, where he was raised on a farm and later attended boarding school. He moved to Melbourne, where he still lives with his long-term male partner. He never considered marriage to a woman and has always been very practical about his homosexuality. He enjoyed a long career as a theatre manager.

Miles, 86
Miles was born in 1931 and lives in Melbourne. He is a very learned man and spent many years dedicating his life to his work in the public service, as well as contributing to community LGBTI organisations. He married when younger, but the marriage was not successful. He did not have any children. He lives with his male partner but has been in declining health.

Neil, 81

Neil was born in 1937 and lives in Melbourne. He also spent five years living in Europe during his 30s. He was a very senior executive with a large staff, so was very guarded about his homosexuality. Nevertheless, he never married and enjoyed his homosexual life. He still has a very active social life, particularly in the music world.

Nigel, 74

Nigel was born in 1943. He grew up in Melbourne and was a public servant during his working life. He travelled overseas for three years when younger. He never married, though he did consider it in his early 20s. He has regrets about the opportunities missed due to the prejudice around homosexuality during his early and later adult years.

Norman, 88

Norman was born in 1930. He lives alone in Melbourne and never married. He was an actor in his early career and later became a theatre manager. He is a quiet and considered man who still enjoys life.

Paul *(Graham Willoughby)*, 75

Paul was born in 1942 and lived for many years in Adelaide before moving to Melbourne as an adult. He married and had a daughter and still has a close relationship with both. He is a gifted artist but has been constrained by indifferent health as he has aged.

Reg, 91

Reg was born in 1926 and lived in Melbourne with his partner of over 50 years. He never married. He was a teacher throughout his entire career and embraced his homosexuality and its possibilities. He was well known and admired in the LBGTI community. Sadly, he has passed away since his interview.

Ryan *(David Bradford)*, 76

Ryan was born in 1941 and spent some time living in Sydney. He now lives in Melbourne with his long-term male partner. He never married. He has spent his career as a doctor and is still very active and interested in LGBTI community, refugees, and the environment.

Rory, 80
Rory was born in 1938 and lives in Melbourne with his long-term male partner. He was a scientist before he retired. He never married. He has strong regrets about opportunities he has missed in life due to the fear instilled by homophobia.

Scott, 89
Scott was born in 1928 and lived in Melbourne. He also worked as a tailor in London for a few years. On his return to Australia, he opened a wool shop and later a florist shop. He did not marry. He was a very religious man but also enjoyed a lively and fun-filled homosexual life with friends. Sadly, he has passed away since his interview.

Spencer *(David Morgan)*, 74
Spencer was born in 1943 and was raised in Brisbane, before moving to Melbourne at age 19 and marrying at 23. He has three children and enjoys a warm relationship with his family. In his early career he was a film editor and went on to become a freelance director, particularly in television. He lives with his long-term partner.

Stephen, 79
Stephen was born in 1938. He lived in country Victoria and now lives alone in Melbourne. He was a reporter in his early life and became an accomplished photographer. He never married.

Terence, 86
Terence was born in 1931 and was raised in Europe. He migrated to Australia with his wife and has a daughter. After his marriage ended he embraced his homosexuality and now lives with his long-time male partner. He was a labourer and later a clerk. He has been in declining health.

Tristan *(Gordon Wilson)*, 81

Tristan was born in 1936 and lives in Melbourne. He spent much of his working life in the hotel industry. He did not marry. He has many happy memories of a fun and exciting homosexual life in the post-war period. He now lives with his long-term partner.

Xavier, 79

Xavier was born in 1937 and lives in Melbourne with his long-term partner. He never married. He established himself in the advertising industry but was always aware of the need for caution about his sexuality. He is nevertheless grateful that he has had a largely happy and contented homosexual life – and continues to do so.

Picture Credits

At a time when even photographs could be used to incriminate homosexual men, it was rare to keep any that might reveal their lives. Some did, though, and we thank them for sharing them with us. We are also grateful to the Australian Queer Archives for granting us access and permission to draw from its rich collection [www.queerarchives.org.au].

Courtesy of the Australian Queer Archives: pp. 4, 77, 78, 79, 136, 139, 142, 147, 151, 164

26, 27 Police Statements, Courtesy of Terry Kennedy ('Bernard').

31 Hawthorn Railway Bridge and Yarra Boulevard, Richmond, 1939, Richmond and Burnley Historical Society HS00052.

82 *The Australian Women's Weekly*, June 12, 1957

99 Courtesy David and Heather Morgan.

122 Courtesy of Mannie de Saxe

131 Freddie Asmussen, State Library of Victoria: H39816.

138 David Lee Bernstein, *Hotel Australia*, Wilkie and Co, 1939.

157 City of Melbourne Art + Heritage Collection

174 https://missiontoseafarers.com.au/history/

Index

A

Adulthood 46, 61, 62–3, 75, 79, 116, 123, 154–5, 163, 180

Adelaide 108–9, 126, 138

AIDS 64–5, 120, 183

Agency 2, 1, 44, 68, 118–9, 158, 163, 185

Altman, Dennis 74, 119, 178, 182–3

Asmussen, Freddy 132–3

Australia/n 1, 3, 5, 6–10, 22–3, 33–4, 39, 41, 44–5, 64, 70–1, 75, 77, 82, 86, 88, 95–7, 102, 114, 116, 118, 120, 125, 130, 132, 138–9, 141–4, 152, 155, 160, 164, 172, 175, 181–2, 184, 187–8

B

Bars 125, 130, 137, 138, 140–5, 151, 153, 158, 166, 177, 181, 186

Barry 54–6, 86–8, 132, 158–9, 170, 172–4

Beats 19, 21, 24, 124–5, 133, 152–3, 158–9, 160–1, 162–8, 177, 180–1

Brisbane 12, 13–14, 101, 108, 138, 145, 162–3

Buggery 16, 33, 44

Bullying 48, 53–4, 61–2, 64, 78, 154, 179

C

Camp (Kamp) 3, 8, 98, 119–20, 126, 135, 182

Celibacy 152–154

Children 9, 21, 36, 59, 62, 65, 68, 72, 74, 79, 80–5, 90, 95–110, 114–16, 153, 186

Coming out 38, 120

Communist 23–4

Communities 4–5, 71, 77, 118–135, 140–1, 152, 158–9, 160, 163, 177, 180–1, 185

Confession/s 17, 21, 25, 28–9, 30, 35, 66, 87

Court 10, 11, 14–17, 25, 31–6, 86, 102, 180, 185

D

Desire 5, 9, 23, 25, 36, 45, 48–9, 50,

60, 66, 68, 76, 96–7, 103, 105, 107, 111, 117, 120, 122, 127–8, 130, 140, 153–6, 159, 160–2, 167, 171–3, 177, 185–6

Difference   5, 10, 45–7, 49–50, 52, 54, 56–7, 59, 60, 65, 70, 76–7, 79, 88–89, 90, 92, 94, 117–8, 150,156, 177, 179, 186

Dowsett, Gary   171

E

Effeminacy   46–7, 52, 54, 59, 61–2, 75, 78–9, 95, 186

Elkin, A. P   81, 83, 96

Ellery, R.S

F

Family, modern, nuclear, postwar, broken   2–3, 5–9, 20, 23, 36, 42, 44, 48, 50–1, 53, 62, 64, 68–9, 72, 78, 80–9, 90–99, 101–9, 111, 114–17, 119, 120, 123, 125, 129, 138, 140, 153, 166, 172, 177–9, 180, 182, 185–6

Fathers   52, 62, 78, 83–4, 93, 116, 179, 180, 186

Fear   3–4, 7, 32, 36, 41, 47, 57, 63–4, 83, 86, 115, 125, 129, 140, 153, 155, 158–9, 161, 171, 179, 180, 186–8

G

Gay   1–3, 6, 8, 19, 21–2, 24, 32, 35–38, 51, 53, 67, 71, 73–5, 86, 89, 91, 93, 98, 100–1, 103, 106–7, 109–12, 114, 118–9, 120, 133, 136–7, 143–4, 146–9, 150–1, 155–6, 159, 162, 166–7, 169, 171, 181–3, 185, 187

Guilt   10–11, 20, 30, 32, 40, 66–7, 79, 86, 97, 101, 140, 153, 159, 160–1, 163, 172, 177, 188

H

Heterosexuality   32, 45, 47, 50, 95, 97, 104, 107

History   1, 5–6, 8, 10, 117, 180–3, 186–7

Hotels   8, 19, 108, 137–8, 141, 168

Hotel Australia   125, 130, 132, 137–9, 141–3, 145, 152

I

Identity   4–5, 8–9, 43, 47, 71, 76–7, 80–1, 91, 95, 116, 119, 120, 127, 130, 136, 181, 183

Individual, the   5–6, 32, 68, 86–7, 121, 124, 178–9, 183–5

Information, lack of   3, 16, 24, 37, 41, 47, 65–6, 76, 87, 93, 117, 129, 130, 137, 143, 179, 180

Invitations 119, 137, 141, 144–6, 152

J

K

L

Language   6–7, 25, 30–1, 33, 47–8, 52, 58, 76–8, 85, 111, 116, 120, 136, 144, 179

Law 2, 8–11, 14, 17, 19, 25, 32–3, 36, 38, 41–2, 44, 81, 89, 131, 142, 144, 153, 165, 174, 176–7, 184–6

Lesbian 2, 61, 86, 91, 114, 182–3

Liberation history/theory 1, 6, 75, 118, 120, 181–4, 187

Love romantic; familial 36, 69, 83, 95, 96–9, 100, 102–4, 122, 124; familial 88

M

Manhood 47, 78, 87, 103

Marriage 2, 5–7, 9, 34, 36, 61, 66, 68, 80–4, 86, 91, 95–9, 100–117, 152, 154, 180, 185–6

Masculinity 8, 45–8, 51–6, 61–2, 74, 77, 80, 116, 127

Medicine, medical 2, 32, 39, 44, 185

Melbourne 2, 6, 17, 22, 24, 31–2, 37, 54, 67, 71–2, 98, 101, 115, 123–7, 131–3, 135, 137–9, 141, 144, 149, 150, 157, 160–1, 165–6

Memory 100, 125, 172, 175, 187

Mental illness , 20, 33–4, 40–1, 50, 54–5, 57, 86, 96, 16, 186

Menzies, Robert 138–9

N

National identity

O

P

Paedophilia 33, 54–7

Parties 4, 8, 65, 73–4, 80, 98, 115, 119, 120, 126, 130, 132, 134, 137, 141–2, 145, 147–9, 150–3, 158–9, 168, 177–8, 181, 186

Partner/s 1, 17, 22, 36, 67, 71, 74, 80, 96, 101–2, 105, 111, 114–16, 122, 140–1, 144, 149, 153, 159, 163, 169, 170, 174, 177

Passing, not passing 3, 46, 48, 57–8, 61, 80, 77

Policing 10, 16, 20, 25

Power 2, 6, 12, 35, 39, 41, 44, 48, 52, 54, 57–8, 60, 64, 92, 95, 97, 104, 129, 139, 163, 173, 180, 184–5

Psychiatry, psychiatrist 37, 39–43

Q

R

Realising 48, 57, 61, 65

Relationships 7, 20, 36–7, 39, 43, 59, 62, 69, 83, 86, 89, 92–3, 97–9, 102–3, 105, 115, 119, 129, 154, 166, 174, 177–8, 179, 180, 186

Religion 2–3, 23, 44, 49, 66, 76, 101, 171, 180, 185–6

S

School 3, 6, 17, 22–4, 39, 46–9, 50–59, 60–2, 69, 71, 76, 85, 93, 154–6, 179, 180, 185–6

Second World War 9, 39, 73, 83, 124, 138, 181–2

Secrets 1, 40, 83, 86

Index   207

Security, national   3

Self   4–5, 7, 44–7, 49, 53, 58, 62–68, 70, 73–77, 80, 88, 91, 98, 101, 104, 108–9, 117, 120, 121, 124, 128, 130, 137, 146, 148, 151, 156, 159, 162, 165, 169, 171, 177, 180, 182–3, 184, 186, 188

Sex, meanings of

Sexuality, and power, and identity

Shame   3, 5–7, 15–16, 20, 44–5, 48, 53, 55–9, 67, 75, 78–9, 84, 86, 95, 112, 116, 125, 155, 159, 169, 171–2, 177, 180, 186, 188

Silence/s   1, 8, 41–2, 52, 64–5, 70, 75, 77, 83, 86, 116, 122, 130, 152, 167, 181, 184–8

Socialising   72, 80, 119, 130, 145–6

Society   2–4, 6–7, 9, 20, 33, 38, 43, 47, 50, 68, 72, 75–6, 80, 83, 95–6, 104, 109, 111, 115, 121, 125–7, 130, 133–4, 138, 145, 149, 151–2, 159, 160, 171, 177, 179, 182, 185–7

Sport   18, 46–9, 50–4, 57, 60–2, 78, 87, 154, 162, 164, 179, 180

Stigma   6, 33, 74, 86, 96, 105, 136, 183

Stories, life stories   1, 3–4, 6, 8, 14, 28, 36, 39, 45, 51, 55, 61, 63, 68, 70, 76, 80, 86, 95–6, 102, 105, 118, 133, 135, 141, 181, 182–8

Sydney   15, 43, 51, 81, 108, 123, 127, 134, 145, 157, 165, 170

T
Truth 5, 187

U

V
Victoria   10, 16, 22, 31, 38, 54, 66, 71, 115, 144

W
Weeks   2, 118, 158, 160

Wife   36, 65, 74, 83, 86, 97–9, 100, 102–5, 109, 116, 122, 133, 135, 160, 166

Willett, Graham   6, 140, 167, 182, 185

Wolfenden Report   67

Work   3, 7–8, 10, 16–19, 20, 25, 36, 48, 63–4, 66, 73, 76, 83, 91, 93, 97, 105–6, 108–9, 112, 116, 119, 120, 127–9, 130, 132–3, 140–2, 145–6, 149, 151, 154, 163–4, 167, 169, 170, 177, 179, 180, 182, 185–6

X

Y

Z

www.ingramcontent.com/pod-product-compliance
Lightning Source LLC
Chambersburg PA
CBHW072001290426
44109CB00018B/2095